# The Living Year

*Mary Q. Steele*

# The Living Year

## *An Almanac for My Survivors*

QUILL

*New York  1982*

**Library of Congress Cataloging in Publication Data**

Steele, Mary Q.
  The living year.

  Reprint. Originally published: New York : Viking Press, 1972.
  1. Nature.  2. Natural history—Tennessee—Signal Mountain.  3. Signal Mountain (Tenn.)   I. Title.
[QH81.S855   1982]     508.768'82     81-22348
ISBN 0-688-00992-1 (pbk.)          AACR2

Printed in the United States of America

FIRST QUILL EDITION

1 2 3 4 5 6 7 8 9 10

*The decorations for this volume, the work of the British wood engraver Thomas Bewick (1753–1828) and members of his school, have been selected and reproduced from 1800 Woodcuts by Thomas Bewick and His School, Dover Publications, New York, 1962.*

To Mary Quintard Steele,
my own dear Maid of Athens,
who may keep my heart

# Contents

# *Introduction*

LIVE IN A mildly rural suburb of a manufacturing town in the southeastern corner of Tennessee. Almost all the events chronicled here took place within a few miles of my house.

When we moved to Signal Mountain, fourteen years ago, this was still a fairly woodsy area. Vacant lots were grown up to weeds and sassafras. Possums trundled in the ditches, at night little foxes crossed the road in the headlights of cars, and toads trilled from every direction in summer evenings. In this short time the trees have gone, the vacant lots have been cleared and built upon, the wet-weather springs dug up and blasted out and rechanneled. Foxes and possums come no more, the toads no longer sing; I must travel miles to hear a whippoorwill. It has been two years now since yellow jackets nested in my yard—those bright harmless sturdy wasps with their tiny-horned goat-heads, which once gave me so much pleasure. My neighbors are relentless—they pour gasoline down the holes and set it afire, they use poison sprays and powders. My children's children will likely never see that lovely curving flight against the shrubbery.

In the woods where I walk, the surveyors every wee
set out their stakes and hack away the undergrowth i
preparation for new roads and new "developments." Th
bulldozers hover in the background, hungry to demolis
the cucumber trees and the laurel slicks and the rattle
snake plantain. The little creek where I once watched th
prothonotary warblers, where the wood ducks nested, ha
had its banks sheared of trees to make room for "ra
relocation." No pretty family of ducks will ever agai
make its quiet way along under the buttonbushes, for th
buttonbushes are gone.

I am no ecologist, leaving such things to the Davi
Browers of this world, for I lack both the knowledg
and the energy for the task. I am besides convinced th
it is a vain effort. Even if we have the means and the wa
to reverse the tide, we lack the will. Something in ma
kind, some worm present when the first anthropoid cre
ture stood up and seized a rock between his fingers and h
apposable thumb, doomed him.

I know what it was like here once, I have seen th
remnants of that magnificence in the Smokies, I know it
useless to hope for its return. But the little ghosts ar
echoes are still with us. I can still look and listen.

To my children's children, then, I would like to sa
This was what it was like to wake up in the morning an
say to oneself, not "Today is Sunday, August 8," n
"Today is the day I have a dentist's appointment or
board meeting." But "This will be the day the cuck
called twice from the hollow and three cicadas left the

) x (

muddy shells on the bark of the hickory tree and the wood thrush sang one last phrase."

It will be a day worth remembering.

*January, 1972*

# The Living Year

# *March*

## ☙ 1 ☙

I WENT UP TO THE wildfowl reserve at Hiwassee Island
to say good-by to the geese. But I was too late. Only a
handful still floated on the water of the inlets, those who
were ill or injured or for abstruse reasons of their own
had decided not to make the long trip to Manitoba. Some
mallards, tidily paired, a few black ducks, a coot or two,
and three blue-winged teal—these were all that were
left of the great flocks and rafts of wintering birds.

The gulls were still there, and the crows. Eight great
blue herons stood about, knee-deep in water along the
edge of the island. Something, perhaps a muskrat, went

zigzagging among them, some creature perfectly aware
that any one of them might stab it with a vast bill and
swallow it whole, and each heron in turn bent its head
with great dignity, with forbearance, to watch this foolish
and frantic progress, as old men watch the antics of children. The twigs of the trees were spatulate with spring.

The geese were gone but I was not sorry to have come.
White-crowned and white-throated sparrows whistled
in the brush piles and a pheasant cackled from the hedge
rows. The day was grey and gradually the clouds lowered
and thickened. When the rain began it did not come in
drops, the air simply grew damper and damper and con-
densed on the lenses of binoculars and telescope until at
last it was obvious that it was useless to stay any longer.

All that qualifies me as a just person is lack of an
umbrella. In truth I rather like being rained on, the less
than subtle reminder that in the scheme of things I am no
more privileged than a frog. Next to life itself, water is
the most astonishing phenomenon the universe has to
offer and rain is its loveliest manifestation.

There may come a day when rain will fall upon the
earth only where technology decides it is needed, and only
when it will provide least inconvenience. Scientists will
order it as they will order the genes of unborn babies, and
men will have become, I think, something rather more
and something a good deal less, than men.

I am almost sure I will be dead before it happens. I
am glad to have come up to say good-by to the geese on
a day when the wind still blew where it listed, from the
four quarters of God's will.

## ❧ 2 ❧

T IS A GREY morning, threatening storm, the trees rock in the wind, their bare branches sing like aeolian harps, the pines and hemlocks roar. And suddenly the wind stops, the day is still, and in the silence I hear the curious small song of a black-throated green warbler, absent-minded, whistling a preoccupied businessman's whistle between his teeth, so to speak, as he plies his trade among the careening treetops.

The warblers are back.

If they were large birds, the event would be less private. By the middle of April when they are here in greatest numbers everyone would know, would look up to see the trees glittering with their brightness. As it is they are such minutive sparks of birds that they can hide behind an oak tassel. Ninety out of a hundred of these shining little birds which come into my ken I locate by voice or by the disturbance created by their quick and constant motion.

One trouble, of course, is that by the time they arrive in throngs and clouds, the leaves are already so far along that even after I have discovered my bird, I often get only a glimpse of it. Though I have been warbler-watching for years there are some of the rarer migrants through

this area that I have never laid eyes on and some th
I have seen only a scattered few times.

In the Smokies near Asheville, I have read, the warble
pour along the mountain slopes, among trees still bare
leaves, flowers, tassels, catkins. Easily seen. Every spring
resolve that I will make the journey, travel to tho
regions where I can stare to my heart's content at the go.
and blue and scarlet and green of all the warblers of t
Eastern United States.

But I never go. That isn't where I want to see n
warblers. I want to see the warblers *here*, in my own tree
my own warblers in my own hickories and hackberri
and behind the tassels of my own oak trees.

# *April*

## ⚜ 1 ⚜

IT IS SAID that birdsong must be learned, each new generation taught by its elders. I wonder when the original composer appeared on the scene and how he went about his first instruction. And I recall all those songs of spotted thrushes in the music of Rimsky-Korsakov, who in all likelihood never heard one.

The lines between artifice and nature are seldom clear to me and technology often blurs them further. Watching television one winter evening, I was delighted to find the room suddenly filled with the voices of hermit thrushes, cool and beautiful and sad and clear. The program was some sort of adventure story laid in the West Indies in winter; the producers were British, and the British are careful about such things. Americans, eager to impress the audience with tropicality, would have used in the background a kookaburra bird or some device purchased in Woolworth's. But the song of hermit thrushes is authentic for that place, for that time.

Today I have encountered another bird on my TV, a flicker on the metal antenna on the roof. He hammers away on the slender pole, producing a tiny metallic whirr. Did he learn this from older woodpeckers, this rolling mechanical equivalent of a song? How long have flickers made use of TV antennae for this purpose? Mine is not satisfactory; he moves to the top of the mailbox, which is better, a wonderfully resonant drum. But it is too close to the road, too open and accessible.

And he ends up in the aluminum gutter over the window by my desk, achieving a triumphantly loud and horrifyingly persistent noise that causes the cat to swell and growl with fear and indignation and makes me laugh. But by and by even my nerves are grated and I move into the living room and get out some Rimsky-Korsakov to put on the record player and drown the sound.

## ⚹ 2 ⚹

IT IS MY WONT to lift the bark from rotting logs and dead trees and stumps to see what I can see. Spiders and centipedes, white and orange fungi, ants, the graceful tunnelings of engraver beetles, bessy bugs. Pick up a bessy bug and hold it close to your ear, and an elf voice says clearly, "Help! Help! Help!" It is rather terrifying.

Sometimes I find a salamander, black- and silver-spotted. So did Cellini's salamander—the one his father called him to see and then struck him so that he might always remember it—go to its fiery death, seeking shelter from heat or drought or cold under the bark.

By the path along the edge of the mountain there is a small section of log whose bark I have lifted and replaced a hundred times. One freezing spring morning three or four years ago I found there a ring-necked snake, stunned with cold, moving only sluggishly in my palm. A lovely small snake, orange-bellied, wearing around its neck a narrow gold collar: I am Mary Q. Steele's little snake, please return.

This spring the log is not there, only the shape of it in a mound of red almost-earth, a richer dust waiting to be concealed. Tiny plants sprout here and there; by summer it will be hidden with briers and daisies; by next spring it will be gone altogether.

## ⚹ 3 ⚹

THIS IS THE TWELFTH of April, the miracle of miracles. Had I been granted the power to work wonders, this is the wonder I would choose to work. How foolish and tawdry and banal other miracles would seem, water into wine, weeping statues, even waking some poor soul from his long sleep. For the world that has grown old and wrinkled and feeble is suddenly made young and vibrant and beautiful enough to break the heart.

What gives these hours their faërie quality, makes their beauty transcend any other, is the poignant knowledge that in addition to being supernatural, they are so brief lived, are going to be gone long before I can really comprehend they are here.

It is the trees. For a few hours, over the hills they are defined in a kind of embroidery, a kind of pointillism, gold, amber, rose, topaz, emerald, rust, crimson, dusty green, honey, scarlet. It will not last a week.

If I lived in a treeless land, no doubt I would make do with something less cosmic, would be content to turn water into wine.

# ☙ 4 ☙

IN A DRY SPRING, cliff swallows gathered mud from the one available wet spot, a ditch along the edge of lawn round a TVA building near Chickamauga Dam. I had ever seen them at this before. They did not come one by ne and take the mud and go away. Rather they hovered 1 the air until twenty or more had congregated and then wooped down all together. Maybe there is safety in umbers, maybe cliff swallows simply like to do things ommunally. Whatever the reason, I did not see any of hem descend to the mud singly, but only in the company f others.

They didn't light. They hovered again, scooping up the aud in those wide mouths, the slim wings fluttering over heir backs. Their eyes have a curious staring look out of heir broad white foreheads.

In this area, at least to my knowledge, cliff swallows ave only in the past ten years started breeding and nest- ng, after the bridge was built over the Chickamauga Dam and lock. They must have spied out the place on nigration, for in the middle of April the power lines round the dam are strung, are beaded with swallows; he air wheels with them, cliff swallows, barn swallows, nartins, tree swallows, rough wings, bank swallows, chit- ering, chattering, burbling, bubbling, flowing through the air like water. Hawks and vultures make of gliding a miracle of engineering, a sparse, stripped, beautiful tool. But swifts and swallows raise it to a work of art, a music of flight, something done simply to gladden the soul.

Under the bridge they fight and shove, hovering to trowel the balls of mud into place, hovering to shoulder aside an interloper, hovering to peer indoors. The bottle-shaped nests crowd close together, and out of the spouts continually look those strange, wide-browed faces.

At Berkeley, when I visited there, the edges of the campus buildings were crusted with the nests, the birds swooped from the Greek theater to the art building and back over the library. "Have they been here always?" I asked, thinking of my own swallows. "Were those nests always here?" But no one knew.

## 5

I WENT FOR A WALK in the spring woods on one of those days, all greenery and glisten, which are almost too beautiful, bordering on sentimentality, redeemed by the certain knowledge of change and destruction. I carried my telescope though the leaves were already so dense that its twenty powers were useless, and I followed a path I have followed a thousand times before. Something in the juices of the day turned me from the trace, to beat my way through the laurel slicks and poison ivy and come at last to a steep bank above a creek. On the far side of the creek a pair of Acadian flycatchers were building a nest, a little woven basket swung out over the water in a fork of branches. The bank was even steeper than I had thought, and my descent panicked a million bean-sized frogs.

The flycatchers were not happy with my presence and sat above my head peering anxiously down at me. At length they went away and came back with some strands of grass, but the time for nest-building had been spoiled, and by and by they began to busy themselves with gnats along the water's surface.

I sat and heard the day slip by in the voices of birds and insects and the sound of opening leaves. In the green creek a gar rose slowly to the surface and looked at me, a glance austere, oblique, and mystifying, like a clue in the London *Times* crossword puzzle. Indigo buntings sang a small catch song from three different directions.

I could not get back up the bank. The telescope was heavy and awkward, the ground was wet. Struggling up, I slid back down.

No one knew where I was. I had strayed a long way from my accustomed road. What traces I had left would vanish in the next shower, due any minute now. Marooned here on this little muddy shelf, I could survive a week perhaps on the green buds around me, provided they were not poisonous. Could I bring myself to catch and eat the new-hatched frogs, the flycatchers, the gar? Could I eat flycatchers' eggs? No Man Friday was likely to turn up.

I am reminded that a friend has recently written me

that she will send her child to "survival camp." She thinks I will be pleased because of my "interest in nature."

She is wrong. I have never felt any compulsion whatever to pit myself against natural forces or to regard them as adversaries. Marooned in fact, I would end up soon enough a heap of bones. Lost in a snowstorm along with many other creatures I would simply die. I am one of those least fit, who shall not survive, according to the rules.

And yet I believe I have a necessary place, a rightful purpose, in this world. When I watch the flycatchers at work, I am, I believe, performing my natural function.

And having reached this conclusion, I pushed my telescope ahead of me and clambered up the bank.

# *May*

## ⚔ 1 ⚔

᠊NATCATCHERS COME BACK early, with the black and
᠊ white warblers. They swarm through the tops of the
k trees, investigating the tassels for gnats and flies and
᠊es and whatever else they can find. They are present in
᠊ch numbers by the middle of April that I am always
᠊nazed that gnats continue to exist in such countless
᠊llions.

Gnatcatchers are rather lovely small birds, but their
᠊tes and calls, peevish and bad-tempered, grate a little
᠊ my ear. Only a hummingbird has a more acrimonious
᠊ice, with a disposition to match. Gnatcatchers are more
᠊aceable by nature, a bark worse than bite. Still, a

crowd of them overhead has an irritating effect on me

Two is different. A pair having some mild domesti
disagreement over a choice of nesting materials is anothe
matter. It isn't, I am aware, bickering—simply commen
and even reassurance; I find it endearing as I watch th
building of that minute cup and the gathering of th
stuffs to make it, the plant downs and stems of fin
grasses, the spiders' silk, and moss, and the lichens tha
will decorate and camouflage it.

Once, superintending such a construction, I grew tire
of standing up and of holding my glasses and eventuall
discovered that the way to observe in comfort was t
stretch out on my back in the mud among the last c
the trilliums and yellow violets, with the gnats swarm
ing around my chin. I don't know how I heard the snake
but I did, and turned my eyes to see him coming towar
me—the long, slender, dark snake we call a racer. H
sensed my presence soon enough and stopped a cautiou
two feet away and reared up a whole ten inches of h
length, licking his tongue in and out, tense, uncertai
After thirty seconds or so he dropped to the ground an
slid away, moving the way snakes move, as though h
had no substance whatever, as flexible as shadow.

I like to remember this little meeting for my luck i
having such a view of a snake. But I cannot help wonde
ing sometimes what he made of the encounter.

# ꕔ 2 ꕔ

THE SPRING RAINS brought down a big dead tree, swept it along the creek and jammed it here, where the banks narrow. And I took it into my head to spend the morning sitting on the log in the middle of the stream.

It was a silly notion. Getting out on the trunk was harder and sitting there far less comfortable than I had imagined. There was nothing to see that could not be seen just as well or better from the bank. But it was pleasant to have the water gurgling around my heels, and the day had had a propitious beginning—a little pale plumy-tailed fox running by the roadside. I postponed for a bit the confession that I had made a fool of myself and sat precariously on.

In the eddies the water was yellow and curdled with pollen; once in a while a cross-vine blossom floated by. A pair of big red buffalo carp thrashed about in some kind of mating ritual among the rocks along the creek's edge. It was going to be, after all, worth my while to sit here and risk falling in.

A little green heron flew up suddenly, squawking as it went, its legs colored a beautiful, sexy orange. A huge mink, ten inches long, crawled out on my log and sat licking its tongue out of its great reddish bullhead and eating gnats. Whirligig beetles spun maniacally on the water's surface, and the air shivered with the fine voices of warblers.

It was prothonotary warblers I had specifically come to see, come to watch them build in a hole in a rotting tree at the water's edge, the brightest birds, with that luminescent, almost fluorescent quality to their plumage so that it glows like that of scarlet tanagers and Baltimore orioles.

The male appeared out of the undergrowth and clung to the bark of the tree. His mouth was filled with moss, his sooty eye stared out of that golden-yellow head. He spied me and was uncertain. But the whole business of the fallen tree was so new and unpredictable that after a minute he gave up trying to fathom the mystery and entered the hole with his little cargo. He disappeared entirely and then shot out again. It was like a light going off and on. He perched on a limb over my head and at length flew off, crying out in a voice as unembroidered and positive as his colors.

Along the bank here I beheld the first prothonotary warbler I ever saw. It seemed then a rare and tropic treasure, as it certainly is, but since that time I have discovered that there are a dozen pairs nesting in these woods. I thought of these birds and of other slow creeks and rivers I am acquainted with and the prothonotaries this May morning building on their edges. It dawned on me suddenly how many thousand of these brilliant slaty-winged bits of birds must be gathering moss within a

adius of a hundred miles of this log, and the thought
as so dizzying I nearly fell into the water. And at last
 concluded that it would be best to go home and leave
 e prothonotaries to their own affairs.

## ⚶ 3 ⚶

THE CATBIRD FLEW into a window and broke her neck
and left one deep blue-green egg in her nest in a
assafras sapling. I could see the nest from the house.
Winds bent and shook the little tree, rains assailed it,
ut for a month the egg lay there until I took it away,
 n spite of its fragility a marvelously tough and efficiently
 haped little device.

Once I came upon a redstart's nest with two young
nes, nearly ready to fledge, tumbling about in it and
 etween them an egg. Not merely an egg which had failed
 o hatch, but an egg which had suffered a mortal wound
 ometime early in its existence so that its contents had
 rained and dried away, leaving it even more vulnerable.
 et the shell remained and was there long after its siblings
 ad left the nest. I went back to see.

## ⚔ 4 ⚔

ALONG THE BANKS of the river and of ponds and creeks turtles cluster like scales on a fish, close and over lapping, to enjoy the sun. Piled one on top of another big ones on little ones and little ones on big, they bask and sleep in the warmth.

But it is not too deep a sleep. Let me shut a car door or appear on the river's edge, or let the sun flash off my binoculars, and they are gone in a series of quiet splashes. "Sliders" we call them locally from this habit, the sleek way they leave the bank and enter the water.

I walked as quietly as I was able to the river, along an abandoned ferry slip, but it was not quietly enough and they went, one after another, from the place where they had been napping on the roof of a half-drowned chicken shed wedged against the bank.

I was disappointed. Not that I couldn't see them as well as I might wish with binoculars or telescope, but simply that it seems foolish not to be able to sneak up on creatures so deeply asleep, so oblivious to anything except the heat of the sun and the sound of the water.

I stood for a while enjoying those things myself, and a small wind, and the new leaves of willows, the squeaks and rasps of grackles and redwings. It was marvelously peaceful.

But something was not right. Something was uneasy-making. Something was there I had not counted on.

At the edge of the weathered wood of the shed a middle-sized turtle still sat, still warmed, watching me out of an enigmatic yellow eye. The thoughts of a turtle, said Emerson, are turtle. And I was disconcerted to find that I had been these last few minutes turtle. He stared beadily on, and after a bit I turned and walked self-consciously away.

## ⚔ 5 ⚔

THE GROUND ROBINS are building in the rosebush. I am reminded of the first towhees' nest with which I was closely associated, a long, long time ago. I could look directly into it from the dollhouse roof, and I climbed up to watch. My children stood below me and said, "Mama, come down!" in scandalized voices.

It is not because of embarrassing my children that I recall the nest, but because of what happened to it. For after the hen bird began to sit, a rogue male appeared from somewhere, brilliant black and white and rust-red, frustrated and demanding. He laid siege to the little household, attacked the male, pursued the female from shrub to tree and back again.

Of the two eggs, one did not hatch and the surviving chick fledged too soon. Fluttering about among the hysterical adults, it fell into the creek and drowned. A somber episode, the destruction of a home, the terror and despair of parents, the death of children.

And yet what I recall are those graceful flights and pursuits, the music of thrushes accompanying a lovely *pas de trois,* and the exotic green and gold evenings of May.

## ☙ 6 ☙

EARLY ONE DAMP MORNING a water thrush flew through the yard; I heard it clicking and knew what it was, and then suddenly, a long way from whatever creek provided its territory, it sang, repeating twice over those three long whistles falling away into a twittering jumble of notes.

Much of bird music, often the loveliest of bird music, is sad: the mourning notes of doves, the burbling self-pity of bluebirds, the sweet, high, melancholy whistles of whitethroats, something wonderfully *triste* in the flutes and bells of spotted thrushes. This song, for all its beauty, is marked by something else, by exultation, by ringing delight. The Louisiana water thrush, that small nondescript bobbing denizen of shadows and wooded creek banks, lives a secretive and unostentatious life. And then unexpectedly that heart-piercing song, wild, outside, untouched, triumphant. Free. Only Canada geese, cuckoos, willets, and some hawks can set my nerves quivering the same way.

## ✹ 7 ✹

CROSSING THE CHARLES, I saw a mallard swimming on the river and at the end of the bridge a Canada warbler singing in a small tree. At Arnold Arboretum there were Baltimore orioles among the chestnut flambeaux, and dozens of yellow warblers in the lilacs. At the Aquarium a laughing gull suddenly appeared among the herring gulls sweeping around the observation windows, and in Harvard Yard a tiny green and copper spider spun the horizontal web it is accustomed to weave in any surroundings, even the groves of academe.

I visit my daughters in Boston, and they are patient with most of my idiosyncrasies. But they fail to share my fascination with the glass flowers in the Peabody Museum, which are neither art nor nature, in their view.

But to have all those delicate innards right here—unfading, easily seen without the interfering aid of magnifying glass or microscope, not stirred by my passionate breath, available at any season—I find irresistible. True, the sight of all that meticulous painstaking, the thought of the hours spent, sets my teeth on edge a bit. I am reminded of circus performers and then uneasily of the stars circling in their courses.

Still I pore over the cases and can go back and look again, any time. And I am ever hopeful of detecting some error, some slip-up, some mislabeling of stamen or pistil. Do the botanists of Cambridge ever visit the place? Would they point out the blunder to the authorities? Or would they, like me, be charmed into silence by the discovery of this relieving human note among the glass flowers?

# *June*

## ❧ 1 ❧

OWN IN THE GRASS and ground ivy we have always a plague of snails and slugs, and after a good spell of damp weather they widen their hunting grounds. I picked seven off one day lily plant and flung them out toward the water hydrant to take their chances with the sun and the robins. Not for anything would I step on them and hear that crunch.

Six of them left my hand and arched out into space. But the seventh had emerged from its shell and clung to my palm. I looked at it, and it was beautiful. The shell was translucent, marbled gold and brown, and inside the creature stewed in its own pearly juices. Bubbles slid

along its length, and it stretched itself toward my finger.
It was itself translucent, the skin grained and grey, bu
underneath the skin I could watch the muscles move. I
turned toward my thumb and extended its head. Th
horns protruded and there, in the back of its head, i
its neck, I could see how it was done: the little containe
of dark liquid that squeezed like a syringe and sent th
liquid out along some channel to make the horn pok
forward. I touched one protrudence; the liquid sho
back into its small vat; the horn drooped and disappeared
into the snail. And then cautiously emerged. My littl
Kyloe Cow explored my hand incuriously from wrist t
the tip of my index finger, a sticky kiss, leaving its silver
imprint. At length I picked it off and put it back on th
day lily and went to wash my hands. Those day lilies
after all, seldom bloomed.

## ☙ 2 ❧

A MILE FROM MY HOUSE I can stand on the edge of the
mountain and look across at a farther edge and see
no house, no road, no power or transmission lines, no
bridge or dam or cut or fill—no sign of humankind. I
like to say it looked the same the day Columbus landed.

I am, of course, lying. If the strip mines don't show,
it is because they are concealed by underbrush or have
blended into the rocks and cliffs, emptied long since of
their resources. The growth along the ridges is thin and
scraggly: post oaks and jack pines and persimmon, sassa-

ras and red maple and black gum, not the vast white
oaks and hickories and poplars, chestnuts and sycamores
that grew here two hundred years ago.

And even now the logging goes on. The scrawny timber
will do for kindling wood, for paper mills. What is today
a wooded hillside can be tomorrow a shaly field of
stumps. The cutting is poorly done, without discretion
and without technique. The roads to accommodate the
trucks are simply slashed into the ground, and, when the
destruction is over, the loggers move off and abandon
their havoc without a backward glance.

Oddly enough, the trees they most often spare are
beeches, left to clutch the rocky and eroding hillside as
long as possible, growing taller and mightier, but only
for a while, doomed like dinosaurs by their own size,
for the thin earth cannot long give them anchorage now
that its own anchorage has been so diminished.

So the road I have meant to take this morning, down
to the river, is blocked by a fallen beech. Like all trees
it has left the ground stubbornly; rocks are still clutched
in its roots and will be for a long time. Under my hand
its bark, smooth and grey as dinosaur hide, is warm,
mobile, still alive. I am filled with one of those sudden,
irrational, totally human impulses to stay the inevitable,
reverse the irreversible. Quickly, while there is time, let
us gather our resources, save this life, straighten this
toppled giant!

The moment passes. Reality returns, logic asserts itself.
Sand sifts down from the roots, the delicate ferny leaves
are wilting. For God's sake, let us sit upon the ground . . .

# ⚔ 3 ⚔

THE WOOD THRUSHES BUILT their first nest of the sea son in the elder bush. It incorporated a good bit c Pliofilm and a large sheet of the stuff was tucked into convenient crotch, laid by for a rainy day, perhaps. Th second nest was in a black gum tree, saddled conspicu ously out toward the end of a bare and almost limbles branch. This nest was constructed in large part of th dead stalks and leaves of last year's cannas; they dangle beneath to a length of three feet and gave the whol business a bedraggled look, like a woman with her stocl ings wrinkling around her ankles.

I heard an uproar in the yard and went out to se what the matter was. A big hawk, a broad-wing, sat i the black gum tree, haloed with shrieking wrens an robins. He was eyeing the thrushes' nest and he seeme unperturbed. But when I came out he took wing and lef flapping off over the treetops with a long tail of derisiv blue jays behind him. I was afraid.

Two days later he came back. There was the san hullabaloo, and I went out once again. This time th hawk sat by the nest, the thrushes moaned in agony, bu it was too late, the little ones were gone.

I was grieved, selfishly, because it meant the end  song. My neighbor's thrush sang for another four week but mine was silent. The nest disintegrated, the long dismal streamers growing forlornly longer as they unwound.

I begrudged those weeks of song, early morning, noon, and night. As much as the clear lovely phrases, I missed the strange little notes that intersperse those phrases— those small stammering, stuttering sounds that are to me as bright and delicate as drops of water falling. For less than four months out of the year I can hear that song. Sometimes a cool wet summer will prolong it into August. And one memorable September I woke for a week to hear it from the woods in the dim morning twilight, an aberration for my private delight.

I could but wonder what the others made of it, for once I had played a record of a wood thrush's song at my window during the fall migration, and from everywhere thrushes appeared and clustered in the trees. For a moment in wonder and in outrage they listened to this April song falling on the October air. And then something betrayed the machine; indifference fell over the audience, they wandered off, and no amount of playing or turning up the volume attracted another.

## ⚱ 4 ⚱

A T THE DENTIST'S I looked glumly out the window—and there was a nighthawk on the flat, graveled roo of the building next door. Dead-leaf shaped, dead-lea colored, almost invisible, mottled grey and brown on th mottled grey-and-brown roof.

It was worth a filling, for I had never seen this before In the country, bullbats are a fairly frequent sight, bu in the city they are seldom more than a presence, a nasa voice above the lighted sidewalks, a rushing dive between buildings. When I see one in the city it is high up, flap ping and soaring slowly, narrow-winged and beautifu in the twilight smog, betrayed by that strident, ugly call

In our cities, in spite of concrete and carbon monoxide life manifests itself surprisingly in any crevice or crac it can discover. But it is strange that so much of tha life is foreign, imported, exotic: rock doves, starling house sparrows; dandelions, chickweed, ailanthus tree gingkoes.

The few nighthawks, the chimney swifts, the occasiona barn owl or pigeon hawk—I value these glimpses of a aboriginal city life. I have little against the newcomer I rather admire their energy and adaptability. I wish however, that I had looked harder and more often fo nighthawks on graveled roofs in days when there was better chance that I should find them. This may be, after all, the only one I'll ever see.

The ailanthus tree is an "escape," a non-native plant brought to this country for cultivation in gardens and then gone wild, spread by seeds or by chance into the parks and fields and woods. "Escape"—I love that word. I see these floral prisoners slyly creeping over the garden wall, gleefully running down the highways and byways, out of jail and into the world, Great God-amighty, free at last!

The ailanthus, the heaven tree, the tree that grows in Brooklyn, has spread over almost all of the United States. Into the woods, but most often into towns. In the driest, bleakest parts of our cities it grows and flourishes, pushing its way between the cracks of sidewalks, struggling grimily up in coal yards, squeezing out of the corners of buildings and railroad bridges, alive and green in a dead and blackened world.

Around the corner from the dentist, someone long ago started to refurbish a run-down building, erected a glass front as a sort of promise of elegance, and then abandoned the project. Inside the glass now an ailanthus tree ten feet tall is confined in a narrow cage, like a circus beast. It presses sadly up against the window and begs once more to be set free.

## ❧ 5 ❧

IN SPITE OF ALL my protestations about not meddling where I do not belong, about being an observer, about avoiding sentimentality, about Nature Knowing Best, I often interfere. I think of some excuse or I blatantly ignore the need for excuses, as every winter I put up and keep supplied a bird feeder, in the teeth of the evidence that it does more harm than good; as I will free the click beetle from the spider's web for the sake of my nerves, as I will divert the ants from this caterpillar, which might (who knows?) develop into some rare and lovely moth.

The cat, who is overweight and inherently awkward, has long aspired to catch a bird and the other day did so, but because of those handicaps muffed it. I ran outside when I heard the screeching, and found the victim, or something less than victim, a young titmouse, just fledged. The cat crouched under a bush and the titmouse struck at her again and again with wings and beak, until I picked it up. Shock had perhaps kept it from flying away, for it was not badly injured, no broken bones so far as I could tell, only a wound on its thigh, bleeding freely. In the house I tried to stop the bleeding with a bit of cotton.

I found in the basement inexplicably a small box labeled Horehound, crumpled some paper in the bottom and wound a nest of ground ivy strands on top of the paper. The titmouse squatted in the leaves. I gave it water from the end of a toothpick, and fed it a mixture of dog food, cornmeal, and evaporated milk. It ate voraciously.

In the morning the little creature was stiffly dead, whether from evaporated milk or loss of blood I cannot say. A small grey mouse of a bird, it was slumped in the wilting ground ivy.

There was nothing else I could have done. Well, I might have left it to the mercies of the cat, or of ants and squirrels and the weather. Death might—or might not—have been then quicker and easier.

But I couldn't have done that, could I?

## ❦ 6 ❦

IN THE LONG TWILIGHT of the longest day I spent a while grubbing weeds out of the border in front of the hydrangea bushes, a task which has for so long included only the interesting middle section that the dull ends have both disappeared under a flood of ground ivy. Once again I worked at the middle portion, which has as one advantage that there is much less to do there. And it had as another on this particular evening one of those chance meetings I will remember with pleasure all my life.

For I lifted my head and there in the quince tree not two feet away sat a young thrush. The bird was suspicious and alert but not truly afraid. Its plumage was still indef-

inite, its tail still something under adult length. It ha
legs like a night nurse, straight, thin and covered in whit
stockings. It watched me out of a liquid black eye an
tilted its head slowly. And I moved slowly closer. I coul
see the white skin around its eye, the small bristly pi
feathers about its mouth, the flicker of breath in its throa

The parent bird spied us, cried out a marvelous note o
warning and the young one went, in an awkward flurr
of panic, bumbling among the branches and diving int
the hydrangeas.

I was not unhappy to see it leave. Who would wan
a longer or closer inspection than I had had of it? Wha
is wildness for if not to make some difference and erec
some barriers between us?

And I remembered another such June evening, year
before, when I had wandered outside and been attracte
to a bush which rattled and shook with birds. When
got within a couple of yards of it, the bush exploded,
vast number of fledgling wrens zoomed out into the air
and in confusion seized the nearest substantiality the
could find. They clung to my hair, my sweater, the bag
ging knees of my jeans. For a haunted moment in th
twilight they embraced that which they had been tryin
to escape. Stricken, neither of us knew what to do. An
then something happened; though I was still frozen, some
thing released them and triggered them into helter-skelte
flight.

## ❧ 7 ❧

*The cuckoo, she's a pretty bird, she sings as she flies.*
*She brings us glad tidings, she tells us no lies. . . .*

SO RUNS A RHYME traditionally sung in our mountains, by people who have no notion what a cuckoo is. They may perhaps have seen a wooden bird in a clock, and they are happy with that. Our cuckoo they call a "rain crow"; it is one of those birds whose call is supposed to presage wet weather.

It is no pretty bird, but a marvelously wild, marvelously handsome creature, with a falcon-fierce set to its head, narrow, pointed wings, and a long white-spotted tail. A silver-bellied slim bird, unmistakable whether flying across the road or sitting in the box elders; and its voice too is totally distinctive, not like any other bird call, a long series of hollow low-pitched notes, growing faster and faster and then slowing again, mysterious and lovely.

Birds not by nature nocturnal call in the night. A brief flurry in the hedges and a startled exclamation or two over some disturbance; a sleepy murmuring phrase, contentment, or memory of contentment, or dream of contentment. On moonlit nights mockingbirds and chats sing and tumble and sing again—for hours while the moonlight lasts.

But I do not know what makes the cuckoo call. On
night as dark as God's pocket that voice will sudden
ring out, resonant and deep, full of magic, haunting th
shadows.

Not song. There is nothing musical about it, really. A
though the bird like the poet had found more enterpri
in going naked.

# *July*

## ⚥ 1 ⚥

HAVE COME ACROSS a new flower—new to me, I mean,
it has been here all along but in the way of humans,
who always suppose they are seeing more than they are,
had overlooked it. And now I have gone scurrying
through my books to put a name to my new discovery.

It is *Amianthium muscaetoxicum,* a tall white spire of
flowers arising from a cluster of long slender leaves. A
native American plant, called fly poison in the forthright
native American way. ". . . a pretty species of Aspho-
delus," William Bartram spoke of it gently, as he spoke
of most things, most of which he saw, since he lacked all
arrogance.

Now that I have seen it and named it I find it ever where, *Amianthium muscaetoxicum,* fly poison, cro poison, bunchflower. I look at it with special pleasure. know its name.

I wonder about this urge to ticket and categorize ever thing I meet. Once I was a bit ashamed of it. If it deligh my eye and gladdens my spirit to see the roadsides with these creamy clusters of flowers, what difference do it make that the thing has a name and place in a botanic key? Suffice to enjoy it.

One of the reasons I am so compelled is communicatio of course. If I tell you of the lovely pink flowers growin by the wayside, you and I are less than equally charme by them. But if you and I both think of marsh pinks grov ing by the wayside, then we have truly shared somethin beautiful, something unique. (Latin names are suppose to take us a bit further, but they don't always. Nomencl turists vacillate like the rest of us.)

There is another reason, a deeper and more diffuse an less easily articulated reason. Perhaps there is somethin after all in the old dark ancient notions of the names power, that some essence resides in a name. Now that have named this plant it is in some peculiar fashion, fro then on, mine. I have possessed it somehow by labeling i *Amianthium muscaetoxicum,* fly poison, a pretty speci of asphodel, in my power.

# ⚤ 2 ⚤

As soon as the first flower appears in the spring, a bee appears to go with it. I think, but I do not know, that the first bees on the first grape hyacinths are honeybees; several people within a few blocks of my house keep honeybees, and so far as I can find out there are no honeybees in my part of the world who do not exist by such tolerance. "Wild bees" are other kinds—flower bees, bumblebees, carpenter bees, leaf-cutting bees. In the abelia bushes they mumble and growl from branch to branch, and though I watch closely I am seldom sure of the species. Simple ignorance accounts for a good part of my uncertainty, and reluctance to pick up a bee and inspect its markings explains the rest.

Bees, of course, are female, or at any rate potentially female. I can with fair accuracy refer to any of these creatures roaring away in the shrubbery as "she." Still it takes an effort. There is something terribly masculine about the way of a bee with a flower. The big burly bumblebees and carpenter bees especially are so awkwardly ardent and impatient, finding the abelia blossom's reluctance to surrender frivolous and worrisome. Often they simply slit the side of the blossom and make an entry, refusing to be bothered with the fuss of forcing their stout dusty gold-and-black bodies into the proper tubular opening, too small to accommodate so large and hard-workir an insect.

These bees are heavy, and if the abelia flowers a beginning to fade, the weight of bee and flower can brir the whole business thumping to the ground amid ang buzzing. And once or twice I have found a bee trapped the more-rich-than-Cleopatra's tomb of a tulip or a da lily, unable to back out of the narrow orifice or to tur around, dead of exhaustion.

Yet bees, one should suppose, ought to be immort: ought to be exempt from death. For are they not t world's only truly innocent creatures? No living thi dies to give them or their offspring sustenance; when th feed they are giving rather than taking life; and whe they resort to their only gesture of self-defense it is an a of suicide.

## ⚜ 3 ⚜

I AM AN INDIFFERENT GARDENER, defeated by my ov ambitions, aiming for delphiniums who should be co tent with phlox. I am, as well, too easily persuaded tl the dandelions and henbit and chickweed are going retain their considerable charms and not turn into sprir ing, sprawling nuisances, cuckoolike shoving the mc legitimate and gentler population out of its rightful be

And I am too easily distracted by any creature which happens along, for instance by the inhabitant of a round burrow here, near the roots of the aconite. If I drop in a grain of sand it will almost immediately come flying back up. If I poke down the hole with a grass stem, moving it cautiously, neither too fast nor too slow, something grabs it and holds on while I draw the stem upward till I can almost glimpse the creature living inside. Almost, but not quite, for the little troglodyte brakes just below the surface, and if I pull any harder, the stem is released.

My victim is a tiger-beetle larva, called by some a doodlebug, but not by me, who came up designating ant lions by that name and still do. A hideous, great-jawed, predacious beast, it lies in wait in its burrow, stoppling up the entrance with its own vast, ugly head, chapped like *Tyrannosaurus rex*. Any luckless insect which comes within snapping distance is fair game. The larva itself is practically invulnerable, equipped with those terrible jaws and a strong hook on one of its segments, which makes it almost impossible to haul it out of its tunnel. There it will hang and gorge its whole one-and-a-quarter inches until winter, when it will close the burrow to pupate and emerge as a full-fledged tiger beetle, a bright and iridescent predator now given wings to compensate for those months underground.

There is a burrow near the aconites this summer as there has been as far back as I have weeded here. There is another among the iris and one in the bank behind the roses, this one so big that I can see those ferocious jaws

flash back from the entrance if I move ten feet away. The
curious thing is that I have never to my knowledge seen
a tiger beetle in my garden in the thirteen years we have
lived here.

## ☡ 4 ☡

EVERY SUMMER I MISTAKE the swifts' small squeaking
voices in the chimney for some unoiled piece of ap-
paratus and am every year provoked at my own stupidity.
After thirteen years I should be prepared.

Yet they are quiet tenants up to that point. In early
April I hear their kissing, smacking twitter and look up
and there they are, three of them, for it is always a *ménage
à trois*. I am not a fussy landlady and have never inquired
into their habits, do not know or suppose I ever shall
know how these domestic matters are arranged.

They are there overhead, a happy presence, the little
bowed black bodies against the sky, the familiar sweet
chippering voices. Once in a while leaving the chimney
they rocket close by as I stand at the top of the back steps.
But for the most part I am scarcely conscious of them,
certainly not troubled by them.

And then it happens. The nest, weakened by rain and
the comings and goings of the adults, gives way under
the weight of the young ones and tumbles to the bottom
of the chimney and then to the furnace flue. The nestlings
come with it. I can open the damper and stare at them

nd they stare back. Their faces are somehow reptilian, r perhaps I should say chelonian: the heads broad and at and the small bills hooked and widely gaping. If the ight catches the skin around their eyes properly, it shines ut velvety Chinese blue.

They scuffle and complain at the bottom of the chimney, nd I worry. I worry that the cats will get them or that hey will get lost in the furnace or chewed to bits in the urnace fan. The parents make frequent fluttering descents ɔ feed them. They will be there a long time, for swifts ʌust be strong and well developed before they start to y. Not for them the primer of short flights from bush to ush. Once they are launched they are almost permanently aunched. They will eat, rest, love, live, even sleep, in heir insubstantial element. When I think the sky is empty f them, I can raise my binoculars and find them circling videly, higher sometimes even than clouds, sustained in pace like fish in water.

Once they were supposed to have no feet, and it might s well be true; what they have are hooks for hanging hemselves in hollow trees or rock crevices or chimneys. ʌeportedly they can hibernate in a real sense, lowering ɛmperature and heartbeat far below normal to keep hemselves alive in a cold climate. They gather their nest- ng materials while flying and glue the twigs together with heir own saliva. In the fall they migrate the huge distance ɔ Peru, swirling and funneling into the tropical valleys.

And then months later they come soaring and fluttering ʌack, in order that I may open the damper and look once ʌore into that singular blue-shadowed gaze.

## 彘 5 彘

THE SUMMER TANAGER has a soft, sadly-questioning, almost bluebirdlike murmuring note. It is an introspective little comment used on occasions that seem to have little in common: on drizzly days, when the tanagers sit in the ivy, idle and hungry; on sunny days, when the wild cherries are beginning to ripen and the caterpillars are plentiful; on hot evenings, when the creeks run dry.

Outside my window I heard that little complaint and saw the male tanager fluttering up under the eaves and went to investigate. The bird was hovering below the roof's edge, dining on the larvae and pupae in a paper wasps' nest attached above the window. The frustrated parents roared and boomed around him, but he was unheeding; so one of them flew down and stung me, for my sins.

It has been my experience that these wasps are possessed of by far the shortest tempers of their kind. Hornets, which have a bad reputation, are seldom resentful of my almost prurient interest in their comings and goings. Yellow jackets, still more notorious, are equable enough, could even be called patient with my interference. Obviously an outsider, but unmolested, I squat to watch them emerge from their burrow, flying off in a long, swift, lovely curve; or to observe them while they police the entrance, carrying

f pine needles and loose dirt, removing leaves, trimming
e grass and weeds for a space of six inches around the
ening, and dumping all the litter six feet away.

I intervene more actively at times. I cover the doorway
ith a flake of pine bark. The bark has a hole in it, and it
kes them only a second or so to discover it and come
it, nervous and troubled. But not about me. In twenty-
ur hours the entrance has been lengthened and deep-
ied below the bark, the flake more or less incorporated
ito the landing strip. I take it away and now the portal
too wide and open, and slowly it is filled in and regains
s original shape.

I put a twig across the way, and it is gnawed to bits; a
af, and it disappears; some moss, and it is disintegrated.
t no time do the wasps seem to associate me with all this
xtra work or to resent my presence. I am seldom threat-
ied, never stung.

And as a reward I close the entryway with a big slice
f peeled cantaloupe. A holiday is declared, and the nest
rges and guzzles; juice drips below and spatters above.
our hours later the cantaloupe is a little wad of dried
ber cast to one side, and the yellow jackets are flying free.

## ⚖ 6 ⚖

UNDER THE MARQUEE outside the grocer's I waited for my husband to come fetch me and shared this umbrage unbelievingly with a fat countryman, sweating but unselfconscious in his Deputy Dawg costume, hired to do a hawking job and doing it.

A mockingbird sang from the top of one of the tall metal towers that provide lighting for the vast parking lot. He caroled and trilled and fluttered and flashed his wings; imitated a cardinal and allowed the imitation to slide into one of a Carolina wren; gave a sudden series of short, sharp, explosive noises; fluttered and somersaulted up into the air; returned to his perch; improvised a few phrases and fell silent.

"That there's a mockingbird," said Deputy Dawg in a voice muffled by plastic and papier-mâché.

"Yes, it is," I agreed.

"And that *there*"—he pointed up—" 's a meaderlark."

"Yes, it is," I agreed, though it wasn't. It was a killdee. It circled the parking lot, flying rapidly and uttering its clear stuttering whistle. Killdees and dragonflies often mistake the darkly shining pavement for water, or at least I suppose that's the explanation for their presence.

The mockingbird began once more to sing. And then suddenly, like a magician pulling a pigeon from a sleeve,

e produced a dove, not the bird's dolorous voice but the
igh sweet whiffle of a dove's wings. I was enchanted.
longed to hear it again. But I didn't. It is part of the
itchery that you have to take what you can get when
ou can get it and learn to like any kind of weather.

"It's hot," said Deputy Dawg thickly.

"Yes, it is," I said, for it was, truly. In a bit my husband
rove up, and I got in the car with the groceries. The
ockingbird sang again as we rode off, leaving Deputy
awg still standing on the sidewalk.

## ⚔ 7 ⚔

A BLACK WIDOW SPIDER built her mazy web behind the
garbage can. She was so beautiful, so glistening
ony-black, so ominously marked with red that I must
eeds go look at her several times a day as she slept, must
ke every visitor to look at her, this shiny lady in her
qualid apartment. She did not endure it long, and where
e went I do not know, though I searched for days.

Alas for my lack of patience and restraint, which be-
ays me all too often. My children found a skink in a
nneled burrow under a flagstone, brooding her five
nall, leathery eggs, the color of dirty sand. Every hour
so I lifted the rock to look at this treasure, this small
ragon standing guard in the sudden hateful sunlight,
er little throat panting in and out. In thirty-six hours
ggs and dragon were gone, and I have never found
other such nest anywhere.

# *August*

## ⚓ 1 ⚓

STRANGERS SOMETIMES TELEPHONE to ask me question
about birds. I am always flattered, seldom helpful.
do not know the dimensions of a bluebird box, or how to
keep sparrows out of attics, or the name of the strange
dark bird sitting in the hickory tree by my inquisitor'
driveway.

For many excited callers I do, however, have an answer
—and a rather dampening one. No, the great red-crested
black woodpecker they have seen is *not* the nearly extinct
ivorybill. It is the pileated woodpecker, a fairly common
inhabitant of this area. A crow-sized black-and-white

d-cockaded bird with an ear-splitting call of lunatic ughter, it is sometimes called "God-amighty bird" or Good-God bird." I am not surprised that people who e it for the first time immediately assume it must be me almost fabled creature.

Six woodpeckers live here the year round, the huge leated and the tiny downy with its larger copy, the airy; flickers and redheads and red-bellieds, all strikingly andsome birds. In winter a seventh arrives, the sap- cker, almost my favorite with its lemon-yellow sides d blood-red head markings.

Every season, every landscape is made more vivid by eir presence and their antics, for they are creatures not together rational by most bird standards, however eager those may be. It comes of banging one's brains t all the time. I have read that woodpeckers' brains are ung on sort of springs to accommodate the hammering, t such an arrangement in itself might produce eccen- cities.

For the most part, woodpeckers, in my experience, efer drinking and bathing in water collected in hollows rotting trees, rather than coming to the ground to ake use of pools, ponds, puddles, creeks, as other birds . The flicker found such a hollow in a black gum the her day, and I watched him splash awkwardly about in a space too small and ill-placed for such a big bird. ut he must have thought it was adequate, for he sloshed ound enthusiastically, and then when he had bathed sat on a branch and preened for a long time. He bent

his head to attend to his belly, and that bright nap
glittered in the sun. A hummingbird came and pend
lumed back and forth over him for several seconds, ove
the scarlet blossom of his neck.

### ☡ 2 ☡

ON HOT MORNINGS the hunting wasps zigzag over th
grass and cluster around the water faucets. I a
pleased to see them, for the strangely graceful, strange
erratic flight that seems to my eye to have no plan whatso
ever, and for the gleaming colors of body and of wing

Several of these wasps have a narrow band of whit
around their antennae, close to the end. Perhaps it serv
as a sort of lure for spiders or caterpillars. Perhaps it
simply there. It makes a bright accent in the glistenin
blue-black or russet.

On these sweltering mornings another insect, a type
big skinny-bodied fly which I have never been able
identify, also hovers and crawls on the grass stems an
mints. The fly also has a narrow white line, except th
this one is around its ankles, on its first pair of legs.
watch this rather nervous creature pausing on a stone
leaf to imitate the wasps. It stands on five legs and extend
the sixth ahead of it—a white-banded antenna. I am ev
reminded of the White Knight—he balances very badl
The attempt to stand on four legs and provide itself wi
a pair of braceleted antennae always ludicrously ends

asco. Without its two front legs, the fly cannot move,
nd sooner or later, after much shifting about from side
o side and foot to foot, it topples on its face.

I think this is a parasitic fly. Its imitation of the wasp
intended either to convince its victims of its innocence
f purpose or to intimidate them into nonresistance. It is
ard for me to believe it succeeds at achieving either of
hese aims.

That design of darkness to appall began, of course, as
oon as life began, the eons-long, painstaking, painful
rocess of arranging things to make being eaten inevita-
le, the immense amounts of energy and time and purpose
irected to one dreadful end. It comforts me a little to
hink of this modest failure, this tiny awkward beast still
umbling about on the hydrangea leaves.

## ⚓ 3 ⚓

OMEONE HAS RUN OVER a possum on the road, and
crows have gathered to scavenge. One of them is a
artial albino; its wings are white, and I smile to see it,
or I recognize it. It has been around the neighborhood
or several years. On the ground with other crows, sitting
n the top of a pine tree, flying along the mountain's edge,
is marked, distinctive.

I hear about albinism a good deal, but for myself I
eldom encounter its victims. One winter, an evening
rosbeak came to the feeder, a male bird with his black

plumage bleached to platinum and the mustard-yellow to cream, an amazing and beautiful sight.

He died in the ice storm that year, and so did the one-eyed field sparrow and the chickadee with the twisted foot and the thrasher who dragged a useless leg. It horrifies me sometimes that these creatures which give me so much pleasure are made individual to me only by being marred or maimed.

## 🐝 4 🐝

A BASILICA SPIDER has built her web in the top of the abelia bush. What I want to know is, where did I first see a picture of a basilica's web so that, at once, the first time I saw it I recognized this lovely small silken pavilion, with its stitch like chain mail, as precise as a snowflake. It isn't in my books; some happy instinct recollected it as first encounter.

The elegant green-and-silver basilica spider, according to all experts, spins her web flat, horizontal. When it is done, she hauls it up like a circus tent by a cable attached to the center. Perhaps she does. I have never seen her do it. I have seen her mend her web, but I have never seen her construct one from the beginning, starting with nothing and ending with this startlingly beautiful structure.

In the long twilights of August and September I can see it done, the building of a similar web right from the

eginning. Not the exact architecture of the basilica, but
n orb web swung in space, ready for its sly work.

All around the house the big brown-and-yellow Aranea
piders, who make their round webs fresh every night
nd demolish them in the morning, live in little huts
nade of silk and leaves or twigs, sleeping all day and
orking all night. Late afternoons they come out, stretch-
ng and yawning, ready to begin. If I am there, and if I
m unobtrusive, I can watch the entire process, down to
ne tightening of the last spoke.

It is pleasant to watch one of these weavers make an
rb, all those legs working so smoothly and busily, swiftly
ut without impatience, hauling, tugging, holding, the
pider circling, circling, swaying, and dipping rhythmi-
ally. But it is the business of putting up the cables which
ill support the final edifice that most delights me. It is a
roject always full of surprises.

Here is the lady who lives in the ivy above the basement
oor. It is a hot, still evening. She stands on the tip of her
y twig, and I think she is considering air currents and
onditions with all the nerve ends of her body. I may be
rong.

She comes to a conclusion, or a beginning. She runs
long the twig, making small struts and guys of silk. And
ddenly she drops and dangles at the end of a two-foot-
ng strand of silk. She hangs in midair and emits a long
reamer of gossamer, and it seeks what breeze there is.
f she is lucky, the wind carries the streamer till it catches,
n the light wire, on the azalea bushes, on the shaggy
unk of the hickory tree.

It is very thin silk. She will now perform an aerial act of great daring and skill, for she will travel along this tenuous rope, carrying in one foot a much stronger rope that she has fastened behind her to the ivy twig. As she goes she will form a living link between this stronger thread and the gossamer, for she has no use for that fragile lanyard and, as she travels, balls it up before her with one of those infinitely convenient pairs of legs.

Again, if fortune is with her, she makes it to the point where the wind has fastened her gossamer, and she herself now sticks down her stronger cable she has brought along. She has laid down the main line. She may have had to make a hundred attempts, frustrated by one thing or another. Mostly she persists, but I have known her to turn around and go back into the house, abandoning the project for the night if it is too wet, too still, or her streamer breaks too often.

On this evening the lady is successful in her efforts and she has accomplished her most difficult task. Now from the far end of her cable she drops on another strong wire and seeks a suitable spot below her on which to fasten the second side of her frame. The ground or grass or the top of a wall or weed or bush, she will not be fussy. She runs about and guys and strengthens this new cable and then she fastens a third strand at this lower point and, carrying it in one foot, climbs back up the second cable and crosses to the far end of her first rope, back to the tip of her ivy twig, and sticks it down. Behold! She has done it. There is a vast silk triangle, the outline within which she will build her round web and

ing herself upside-down to wait for moths and beetles.
I find it always a surprising and amazing contrivance,
ie of those things I would never have divined for myself,
oking at the finished product, never have devised for
yself had I been born to that station of life. I can watch
again and again, and never find it boresome.

The little engineers are aware of my presence, often.
I come too close, they will stop—dead-still for a second
two—awaiting my intentions, but if I make no hostile
ove they go ahead with the work.

One night, idly watching this lady over the basement
oor as she waited for her gossamer to cling to something,
was a little taken aback to see her come scrambling
ward me. It took me a moment to realize that the
reamer had indeed adhered to something—the top of my
ead. I jerked away, a little frightened by her rapid
pproach and not wanting to stand all night supporting a
ider web.

But I was flattered out of my mind to have been taken,
gainst all odds, for a natural object.

## ⚞ 5 ⚟

N THE DRY BED of a wet-weather spring I came on the
skeleton of a lizard, or perhaps salamander, I do not
now. What brought it to dust I haven't the faintest
otion, but whatever it was had left it extended quite
aturally on the sandy stream bed. Not a shred of flesh or

skin was left on it, only the marvelously articulated little pale bones, wonderfully jointed and fretted, and the long line of its tiny vertebrae, like the links in a carved ivory chain.

"Discerptible" is the word that comes into my mind, an old word that has always made me think of serpents and herptiles, for obvious reasons, and now will seem more fitting than ever. "Discerptible," capable of being disjoined, an ancient word worn out and disused and stripped of every connotation as the lovely small spinal column here is stripped of all its flesh.

## 🙵 6 🙵

I HAVE NEVER USED a poisonous spray in my garden. Long before *Silent Spring* I distrusted such things and anyway I am in truth as attached to the six-legged beasts who inhabit my borders as I am to the flowers. Planthoppers, it is true, have some years damaged my variegated Hostas. But it has been worth it, to see the nymphs dressed in their flocked, feathery white skins, like infinitesimal bits of cotton candy; to see the strands of trumpet vine keeled with long lines of pale green adults, one directly in front of the other for the space of a yard.

Grubs were responsible for the deaths of a whole row of bellflowers early this summer, but my sorrow at the loss of flowers was most assuredly assuaged by the sight of

une bugs hovering over the grass, by the fascinating
)ectacle of a rhinoceros beetle crawling along the porch
oor.

The natural enemies of such creatures are present here
a vast numbers: shrews, moles, birds, lizards, spiders,
mbush bugs, assassin bugs, wasps, parasites, fungi, mi-
robes, viruses—the list is endless. Surely no insect in the
orld can survive to maturity and continue the species,
nd surely and abundantly every species goes on—one
f life's long unhurried series of rather grubby miracles.

In February, in the woods, I found a Chinese mantis's
gg case and brought it home out of curiosity and stuck
in a Nandina bush, not knowing nor very much caring
hether the eggs had already hatched. In May the day
lies were suddenly swarming with apple-green, inch-
ong, sticklike little creatures, dining as often as not upon
ach other. They shed their transparent skins, little ghosts
f mantises perfect to the last tooth of the smallest claw,
mong the columbines. As they dwindled in numbers they
ncreased in size, the green more and more submerged in
arm leaf-brown.

Four are now apparently permanently established in
ae border, monstrous four-inch eating machines, marvel-
usly disguised, hanging upside-down from the heads of
hlox, with their huge serrated forearms cocked and
riggered. The one just below the porch I watch most
ften.

When I come close, her small triangular head whips
round toward me. Her compound eyes, green and trans-
ucent as the flesh of grapes, watch me intently, but if I

am quiet and do not move about she very shortly lose
interest. A bee bumbles among the blossoms and sh
lunges, the enormous forelegs piston out for the bee, but i
escapes. She does, however, catch and eat many bees
sometimes quite large ones. Is she too well armore
against the stings? Or immune to the poison? I do no
know.

The bee departs, and a small, green, long-horned grass
hopper leaps within range. She has him, effortlessly
plucking him out of the air into those merciless gin traps
He is shackled in her strong legs, impaled on the spikes
helpless. She bites him on a small haunch and I hear hi
silent screams. Then she bites into his head, on the secon
or third mouthful his convulsive struggles cease, thoug
his legs jerk reflexively on. She eats with greedy relish
lip-smacking over every morsel. She eats all of the grass
hopper except one thin striped antenna that falls lightl
to the ground. Then she cleans herself meticulously
going over every one of those murderous hooks for the
last crumb, whether out of gluttony or fastidiousness i
hard to say.

Every few minutes from dawn to dark, perhaps even
through the night, she repeats this Grand-Guignol per
formance. And yet I find that it is possible to think of her
with something like affection. Waking in the night to a
great windy storm, I hope she has found some protection
from the pouring rain.

# *September*

## ꗛ 1 ꗛ

ˑT IS VERY HOT, and we have had no rain for nearly two
. weeks. The jarflies rasp all day, the katydids make their
accato accusation all night. The earth cracks and the
ery leaves sweat.

I turn on the water so that the sprinkler plays over
ie leaves of the dogwood and bridal wreath—and in
inutes the place swarms with birds, every kind of bird,
icluding the first of the migrants, warblers, rose-breasted
osbeaks, orioles in their dusty-looking fall clothes.

It is the best way I have ever discovered to attract birds.
ven in weather not so dry they will come to the sound of
ater falling, as I would myself. There are some people

who claim that birds can be drawn close to the watch‹
by such means as "squeaking on the back of one's han‹
or using some mechanical device. Perhaps I don't unde‹
stand how it's done, for it has never really worked for m‹
Except once.

One spring in a thin woods I tried luring the warble‹
out of the treetops by "squeaking." They came in flock‹
in such agitation and fury that I was taken aback ar‹
stopped. And after a bit I discovered sitting over my he‹
in his pride of place an interested duck hawk. It was h‹
presence, not my talent which had drawn the birds.

But there for a moment I had rather fancied myse‹
as a bird charmer.

## ⚔ 2 ⚔

IT RAINED THE FIRST two days we were at the beach, ‹
the South Carolina coast, and the second night the‹
was a storm, a great wind and rain off the ocean, so stro‹
it leaked around the edges of the windows and dripped ‹
puddles from the sills. The next morning it was gon‹
the sky was blue and cloudless, the waves long and va‹
and smooth. At the north end of the island there was a b‹
tidal pool, a rare thing here where the beach is all sil‹
sand.

It was full of creatures. Dime-sized crabs, tiny flounde‹
(so young they still swam upright with their eyes prope‹
one on each side of the head), small, ugly fish with gre‹

butterflylike fins spreading out from beneath their chins,
finger-length squids with eyes of a clear baby blue and the
most incredible malignity, an infinitesimal starfish, and a
multitude of hermit crabs and shrimplike beasts, which
I presume were really shrimp.

The little pool was an execution chamber. High tide
would never cross the forty-two feet of slope to the edge
of the pool. The sun was hot, the water level sinking.
My son had with him two aquarium nets, and we found a
rusty can. For two hours we chased and netted. The squids
uttered small harmless oaths of brown ink, and the crabs
industriously buried themselves. A least sandpiper, pro-
portioned to the other fauna, an exquisitely minature
edition of its larger cousins, scurried at our feet and once
or twice was rewarded with a crab or shrimp.

The sun was hot, bending and squatting became painful, the last of the little creatures were slippery indeed,
frantically hard to catch. But the pool was emptied.
Everything but the tiniest and most elusive shrimp or
whatever had been transported back to the ocean.

My son said proudly, "It makes it almost worth while."

My back ached piercingly. We were late to lunch,
incurring the wrath of the lady who ran the inn, who had
already taken against the length of our hair and the cut
of our jib. Ninety per cent of the rescued fish had long
since, I felt sure, fallen victim to one of that series of
mischances that constitute life, in the ocean or on land.

But I had to agree. It made it almost worth while.

## ❊ 3 ❊

W HEN I VISIT the seashore, one of the books I alway
take with me is a fat, green, boxed volume calle
*South Carolina Birdlife*. It is the queen of bird book
handsomely illustrated with paintings and photographs s
evocative of the Low Country that I can hardly bear t
shut the pages; crotchety and full of a kind of fierce, lovel
jingoism: few birds have been able to resist the urge t
visit South Carolina.

But the feature that attracts me most I have neve
encountered in another state bird guide: a purely gratu
itous rendering of the Latin names of the avifauna int
English.

Thus the common starling is listed as *Sturnus vulgari*
which the authors dutifully translate as common starlin
without comment. Nor have they anything to say abor
the Florida grackle, "*Quisculus quiscula quiscula* (a qua
a quail a quail)" though an error twice-compounded d
serves some notice, I would think.

Once in a while they provide a helpful addition. Th
lapwing, for instance, is denoted *Vanellus vanellus* an
the reader is informed that *vanellus* means a little fa
in reference to the winnowing noise of its wings. Th
subspecific name of the belted piping plover is *circu*
*cinctus* which is translated as "surrounded, *i.e.,* belted

And they are moved to remark the endearing appropriateness of *Clangula hyemalis,* a little winter noise, for the old squaw.

But they maintain a stiffish silence about such flights of fancy as "*Capella gallinago delicata* (a star in the constellation Auriga, a hen, delicate)" for Wilson's snipe. Or for the gull-billed tern, *Gelochelidon nilotica aranea,* "a laughing swallow of the river Nile pertaining to a spider."

I am myself charmed and delighted by some of the names; by *Chordeiles minor,* "a smaller evening musical instrument," for the night hawk; by *Bombycilla cedrorum,* "the silky-tailed inhabitant of the cedars," for cedar waxwing.

I am more than charmed, I am in fact reassured. I am distrustful of scientists, not altogether certain I want to go where they seem to be taking us. It is encouraging then to come upon this streak of poetry and imagination in the cold of the laboratory. There must be some redeeming qualities in the cast of mind that devised the name *Calidris canutus rufus,* for the American knot, the reddish sandpiper, up to its knees in the waves, vainly commanding the tide to halt. I like the humility that so often often comes up with names translating simply "some bird" or "an unknown bird." And oh, the dreaming magic of *Dendroica petechia aestiva,* the tree-dwelling, island-loving Eastern yellow warbler, pertaining to summer.

## ⚔ 4 ⚔

TEN MILES UP THE BEACH is Huntington State Par and Wildfowl Refuge. Its road leaves the highwa and winds through sand and tall pines and eventual becomes a sort of causeway. On one side, a marshy lak edged and ornamented with cattails and other reeds, ar on the opposite side, tidal flats and sand bars, trimme with sandpipers and oyster shells, stinking gorgeously mud.

We went one misty morning when the tide was near out, when the wind barely stirred in the grasses and tl water gulped and belched among the sand bars. Ter circled overhead; around the lake, egrets and hero dreamed; a least bittern, straddled between dried stalk watched us intently. Coots and Florida gallinules ar even a few purple gallinules floated on the water.

Some official of the park dumped a great, greasy lun of offal into the water, to attract the alligators. Tl alligators, surfeited with coots, slept on, drifting amor the pond lilies. But huge crabs evolved from the shado and excitedly began to pull at the meat.

Across the way dowitchers and night herons walk solemnly about. A fleece of fiddler crabs heaved over tl mud and ibises stitched, stitched, stitched away, probi with those enormous curved bills.

Four black skimmers come barking among the sand
bars. They come so close I can distinctly hear the sound
made by those great beaks cutting through the water.

My son walks along the edge of the lake and a long
shape rackets into the water under his feet. He turns
toward us a face almost green with excitement. "Jesus,"
he says in awe. "I stepped on an alligator."

My children share to some extent my love of and excitement for this section of the earth. But they have been
here less often than I had at the same age, and anyway
their experience and their passions are less limited than
mine have ever been. For me this is a landscape stained
and scented with romance. Every line of it is heavy with
nostalgia for the enchanted hours I spent in these marshes
long ago.

But I never made this country my own. My visits here
were short and separated by a year or more. No matter
how intensely I cherish and cultivate it, it remains as
exotic as the moon. When I leave it behind I cannot but
suppose it disappears, like a travelogue film spooled back
into its can.

## 5

ONCE, WHEN I CAME to this shore, pelicans—morning
and evening—made their way, half lumbering, half
gliding, half awkward, half beautiful, over the water to
their feeding places. Where the tidal inlet, known here by

its old name "creek," flows over the sand they sailed an
bathed, capsized like ships in the current, in all thei
ugly glory.

Once when I came here ospreys presided over th
beaches; every hundred yards they flew and circled, crash
ing into the water like falling stars. Above the reed
grasses of the marshes pair after pair spoke to each othe
in ringing voices.

I have not been here on the coast in several years.
had been warned about the push of pollution and pest
cides and human destructiveness. I saw no osprey in
week and one string of seven pelicans.

## *October*

### ❧ 1 ❧

BY THE END OF SEPTEMBER the titmice and chickadees have gathered in the japonica outside my window to remind me that it is time to put up the bird feeder. They fuss about in the shrubbery and along the sill, and at length I do get out the feeder, which is old and broken and caked with accumulated droppings and peanut butter. But it's what we are used to, the chickadees and I.

Still, almost always, the first to venture in is a Carolina wren. For wrens of any species, the world consists of suitable holes for nesting and then the grey anonymous rest. Even a dilapidated bird feeder will be inspected.

Any reasonable opening anywhere and they will squeez
through, and will even bring in a few half-hearted gras
stems. In December I watched a nuthatch trundling alon
a dead limb until it came to a hole, where it stopped an
peered in. Nuthatches, also, are interested in holes, bu
more exclusively—only in holes in trees. After a momen
the nuthatch moved on but then in a bit turned back an
once again leaned over and stared into the hole. And ou
flew a wren, indignant, feathers ruffled.

I am less than happy about wrens nesting on my plac
They do it so continuously, from February to Octobe
And while they are nesting they are driven to nerve
wracking screaming at cats, jays, crows, squirrels, star
lings, or pieces of newspaper. I try to be firm abou
nests in the garage, keeping the doors closed, callousl
removing half-finished nests, taping up cracks and hole
But I never succeed. Somehow they get in. Somehow the
hide the nest away until the eggs are laid, when I canno
bring myself to break up the housekeeping; sometime
they deviously even make use of last year's nest. The da
will be made hideous with their racket; the young one
being so numerous, must think of new and more efficien
methods of limiting their numbers, will drown in th
dog's water, get run over by the mower, throttle then
selves in places their already strong holing instinct force
them into.

A nest in the mailbox is worse, a time bomb set to ki
first the postman and then the addressee, a stage fo
heart-breaking tragedies. And yet at five o'clock on

dismal January evening, how has my soul delighted to
hear that loud, brave whistle, that song made cheerful
by the irrefutable knowledge that there is no other way
to be.


## ☙ 2 ☙

THE UGLY, RUTTED, abandoned mining roads, running
sores on the sides of the mountain, switch back and
forth under the cliffs. The roads do far more extensive
and far more hideous damage than the mines themselves.
The one I travel this day is surely and steadily causing
a whole great section of the mountainside to slide away.

Still the trees and shrubs hang on impossibly. And from
the first of March till the middle of November the hurts
are covered with greenery and flowers. I have never seen
anywhere such numbers of spring flowers, such sheets of
bloodroot, that paradisiacal flower, the first, the most
perfect. Hepatica and anemones and trilliums of all kinds,
jack-in-the-pulpits, fire pinks, Indian pinks, devil's-bit,
goatsbeard, butterfly weed, Queen Anne's lace, goat's-rue,
bee balm, ten varieties of ferns—out of the starved and
rocky earth they boil up in a long river of leaves and
blossom.

The flowers of October are smaller and coarser and
less lovely than the flowers of April, but not less abundant.
The edges of the road are buried under a froth of asters

and boneset and joe-pye weed, goldenrod and monke
flower and gerardia.

Scrambling down the trail I remark also that th
scents of fall are less subtle and even more numerous tha
those of spring, wonderfully pungent smells of wet eart
and dry leaves, of many mints including the sharp, strong
lemony smell of richweed, of a thing like curry from som
source which I have never identified. And while I ar
crouched there sniffing, something happens, somethin
lovely, something strange.

The edge of a cloud-shadow passes over, slipping acro
my arms and shoulders and head like a cloak fallin
behind me. I have been in shadow and am now in
second in sunlight. An unbelievable thing, that so fa
away and insubstantial a body should have so touche
and changed a walker on this hillside, as uncannily as
year slips over the mountain, changing hepatica to hawl
weed and back again to hepatica.

## 3

OCTOBER FOR THE MOST PART is a limp and lacklust
month here. The oaks still keep their green, but th
leaves are dull and dry; no amount of rain will mak
them lively, will wash away the dust.

Bloom is sparse and hesitant, woodpeckers cry out, th
pears thud to the ground and their bruises ferment. Th
wasps and yellow jackets carouse on the juice and the

lie about on their backs giggling and kicking feebly. The
days are mild, hazy, and shadowless; the nights are tame.

But evenings are another matter. Then the air is clear
and yellow, tinged with bronze. Among the oaks the out-
lines of more precipitate trees take on a new grace and a
new emphasis. Reflected from their fallen leaves, the light,
strong, sad, uncompromising, comes strangely up from the
ground.

## ☥ 4 ☥

HUMPING ALONG the flagstones is a caterpillar, the
larva of a geometrid moth, so called from the strange
wooping method of locomotion employed by the caterpillars. The earth-measurers. Inchworms, of whom my
insect guidebook says solemnly: "There is considerable
evidence to support the prevalent belief that the finding
of a measuring worm on one's person presages new
raiment."

This is one of those caterpillars which resemble twigs,
greyish black in color, knotted and knobbed, slightly ir-
regular in outline. Reared up stiffly straight it is remark-
ably twiglike. So might it have escaped by this device all
enemies but two.

For this caterpillar has been parasitized. Along its back
are ranged seven small white cocoons. The caterpillar is
shriveled and dull. The marvel is that it is still alive at
all, for little of its own substance remains, since it has

for some time been providing a still-living meal for the wasp children attached to its back.

The second enemy that will have its way with the caterpillar, disguise or no, is, of course, the weather. The caterpillar was late emerging from its egg. The wasp was late in finding it, to deposit her eggs upon its skin. Their presence has slowed its growth, already perhaps inhibited by difficulty in finding the proper food. The caterpillar will not pupate. The tiny wasps will not draw the last ichorous mouthful from their host. Frost hovers in the air. Before long both little murderers and victim will feel the cold weight of its equable hand.

# *November*

## ❧ 1 ❧

I LOOKED UP and there in the clear blue-and-gold evening sky hung a great weather balloon, high, cold,
onely, glowing in the light of the setting sun, wrinkling
n some extraterrestrial wind.

Nothing that I could see shared the heavens with that
nachine, not even a late last starling, no wisp of smog
or cloud. It moved slowly toward the earth's rim—far
out there. Up there? Where?

Astronomers must be, I think, most extraordinary
beings. I cannot for more than a second or two contem-
plate that enormous and appalling vastness, that which
has no beginning and no end, no time, no dimensions,

is not *contained* in anything. I shivered now from more
than cold and, stepping back into my house, was grateful
for more than light and warmth, was grateful for this
little minute, this blink of time, in which to be something
else than stars and stones.

## ⚓ 2 ⚓

CUT OPEN A HYACINTH BULB—who would dare?—and
it is said you will find already perfectly formed the
stalk of flowers waiting for spring. The seasons are contained, one within the other, in an endless series of
Chinese boxes; this year's bud holds next year's blossoms,
this spring's egg holds every egg that has been and every
egg that is to be. In July the dogwood's leaves are
turning and the buttons of April's blossoms are already
forming.

In November, in the middle of a rocky path, I found
a tiny clump of bluets blooming, pale and fragile, under
a cold and stormy sky. I dug it up and brought it indoors
and it bloomed all winter long, sending up smaller and
smaller buds on thinner and thinner stalks until spring
came, when it softly died, consumed by the effort to
rectify its error.

## ✕ 3 ✕

THE DAYS GROW SHORT and the nights are cold. The yellow jackets no longer come to scavenge from the at's dish. The entrance to their burrow under the forythia bush is no longer kept clipped and tidy, grass grows on the runway, few wasps come trundling up the hole into the open air. When they fly, they fly with the old bright energy and directness, but often they spend a long time clinging to the grass stems before they take off. Their colors are dimmed, their wings bedraggled. Sometimes they cling all day and at evening I find their sad little corpses by the doorway.

In 1895 someone brought to this country from the Orient the kudzu vine to shade and ornament gazebos and porches. I do not know when it was first used to prevent soil erosion, to cover cuts and fills. But it proved excellent for the purpose, growing rapidly, putting down numerous roots, and keeping its foliage late into the year. In this region, where the climate suits it, it has become a pest, crawling and sprawling over the waysides, impossible to get rid of. It even swallows huge trees and turns them into green mastodons grazing across the hills.

In the night we have had a hard frost, and the behemoths have died. Though they still stand, they are scorched and blackened. In the cold wind the dead leaves turn and twist like tag-ends of burnt flesh and skin.

Under the forsythia bush the yellow jackets' gateway has begun to crumble, and all day long the tunnel is empty and no small wasp comes forth.

## ⚜ 4 ⚜

I WENT TO THE wildfowl refuge on Hiwassee Island to see the geese. I don't often go during the season, not wishing to run the risk of being shot. Not wishing, either, to see the geese shot. Besides, the gates of the refuge are closed and locked; so I must climb the high bluffs and look down on the river and the island. It was a grey day with a cold wind, and the geese would not move, would not get up and fly, would only squat on the sand bars looking off toward the mountains or, in the water, tip up, showing their white petticoats and revolving slowly head down. They would not even speak, only here and there a single bird honking, not the lovely, wild, bugling chorus of a moving flock, the deep, sweet, spine-tingling music. One of the reasons I don't go up on the cliffs very often is that once or twice I have been so caught up in that rush of wings and voices above my head that I have nearly gone over the edge—a clumsy and rejected Leda, come near to putting off anybody's knowledge or power.

Below the cliff a great blue heron swept by, croaking
to itself in its toad voice. I squatted by my telescope.
Across the river a man in a small boat tended a trotline, moving from one floating plastic bleach jug to the
next one, hauling up the empty hooks. When he leaned
over, his jacket slid up his back revealing several inches
of bare flesh. In the trees winter birds moved about:
myrtle warblers, purple finches, a winter wren, a fox
sparrow. In a bush by my side a small brown spider
tidied her web, tightening a guy wire here, a stray cable
there, dropping some tiny carcass wrapped in silk. Mid-
November is late for spiders to be about—by my reckon-
ing, not hers. While I watched her some ducks flew by,
talking among themselves in little purring, crooning
notes. I never knew what ducks they were, but I have
never forgotten that soft murmur; if I ever hear it again
I shall recognize it.

Close to this place is a dead tree. In the years I have
been coming here it has lost every branch and now stands
a stark pole, ready to break to pieces in the next storm.
Woodpeckers often hitch up and down it while I sit here
waiting for the geese, but on this day a big red-tailed
hawk perched on its top, looking down at the river with
the gaze of terrible anguish that hawks can wear. I sat
watching him, and after a moment he turned his head
and watched me. When he left, the dead tree swayed
back and forth for a full thirty seconds in reaction to the
thrust of his feet.

Coming down off the hill carrying my telescope, it
occurred to me, as it had a hundred times before, that

I am one of the lucky ones. This is all I have so far in my life wanted or needed. But I cannot help wondering what will become of people like me when the world is cemented over.

# December

## ℥ 1 ℥

ABOUT A DOZEN cardinals have come to my bird feeder this winter—and one of the males has lost his tail. From being a bird of some presence and dignity he has been transformed into a silly and Disneyfied creature, almost round, a rosy-red ball among the privet leaves.

Every winter I notice a number of birds who have suffered such a loss. In subfreezing weather tails freeze to roosting places and the feathers are left behind when the bird flies up to break its fast. Or at least so I surmise. The curtailment makes an astounding change. Sparrows become quaint and quail-like; the thrasher looks grotesque as well as mad—that lunatic yellow eye; chick-

adees dwindle unbelievably, and their dark heads make
them seem top-heavy, as though they were going to topple
on their faces at any moment; a tailless titmouse on the
ground looks more like a large grey beetle than a bird.

In the case of the cardinal I suspect a cat, for we have
had very little frost so far this winter. Nevertheless the
birds, influenced more by hours of daylight than by
temperature, behave as if the weather were cold. By four-
thirty the yard on the west side of the house is filled
with birds, for on the west the trees and the house itself
are covered with ivy. Juncos and wrens and cardinals
fly in and out, discovering the safest and warmest sleeping
places, jealous of corners and crevices. They burrow in
and flutter out again to take a final drink, inspect a better
site for sleeping, eat a last berry. Waxwings whisper
nervously from the hedge—but I have never seen one of
them enter the ivy to sleep. A sapsucker swings from a
long branch and calls and calls, and eventually another
bird appears—what is it? I cannot tell against the sunset
sky—and they both fly in among the heavy leaves. A
mate? Or just a friend? Or simply a bird that showed
up coincidentally as the woodpecker made up its mind to
retire?

By six, when the last light is fading, they are all abed
warm in their feathers, sheltered by the greenery. Are
they asleep? A still-restless crow lands in the top of a
black gum tree and calls out a series of insolent croaks.
The tree's flesh of ivy ripples and crawls with outrage
for a second, and then the winter night settles down.

# ⚔ 2 ⚔

MY EDITION of the *Britannica* is ancient indeed, many of the volumes have lost their covers or even the first or last few pages. It is supposed, nevertheless, to be a good edition, and I find it useful. I took down a volume to look up FUNGUS and, appropriately enough, the spines are so mildewed that at first I chose the wrong one. In discovering my mistake I was waylaid by FALCONRY and FLYING, with pictures of biplanes and triplanes and surprisingly even a monoplane, and I spent a few moments with FENCING and a thoroughly confusing biography of EDWARD FITZGERALD.

The spine is missing from the proper volume, and I opened it at GILGAMESH and flipped back to GEOMETRY and then to JOHN GAY. I read the whole article on GAWAINE and came at last to FUNGUS.

I was looking up FUNGUS to discover if there is some general category for soft and ephemeral kinds of fungus like puffballs and mushrooms as distinguished from hard and long-lasting woody kinds like horseshoe fungus and other shelf fungus.

If such a distinction is made, I did not find it in my encyclopedia. There was a good deal about penicillium, our uses of which were not then known. The discovery that lichens were symbiotic arrangements of algae and fungi had been made such a short time before that it was wonderingly commented on in the article. I got lost among the rusts and smuts and closed my volume briskly enough to dislodge another page.

Outside we have had a week of mild weather here in early December. Whatever their designation, mushrooms and puffballs have sprung up in hundreds. The woody types, of course, are still around as some have been for years.

I went poking among the toadstools, about which I know little or nothing. These I can identify as morel and that as boletus. And this one coming up here is some kind of puffball? I touched it with my foot, miscalculating, and stripped a big flap of skin from the round ivory top protruded from the earth. The flesh was moister and more translucent than a puffball. I knelt to look, and, to my consternation, the thing slowly but surely levered up that slice of skin and lowered it back over the shivering pulp.

I was troubled by this sight, which seemed to me an occurrence that should not have taken place, if it really did. I went next day to look at it again, but I could not find it.

# *December*

## 3

NO MATTER HOW COLD the weather, life still persists in my basement. Spiders, small round, brown house piders and long-bodied, pale mysterious ghost spiders, ang in the windows or under the furnace pipes; slugs eave a glairy path across the concrete floors; cave crickets eap joyously from the corners.

But the creatures whose presence astounds me most are aterpillars, the rich-colored, furry-coated "woolly bears." hey sleep curled up in drainpipes or crevices or under eaps of rags. Disturbed, they unroll and trudge off, head own, like a stubborn child, searching for some other eaceful place out of harm's way. Their black and brown nd tawny coats are dimmed with dust and lint and bits f cobweb, but they themselves seem in good health.

Some butterflies hibernate in mild climates. Some utterfly eggs survive the cold months in sheltered loca-ons. Most members of this insect order winter as pupae, 1 cocoons or chrysalises. Except for woolly bears, I don't un across caterpillars in winter.

And it is not only in my basement that I find them. rubbing about in the fallen leaves and dried weeds f my flower borders, I sometimes come upon this furry ersonage. The world is full of surprises. Three or four mes I have picked up such a woolly bear to discover that it was stiff and dry, but under the dark gold pelt the pupal case was hidden away.

Caterpillars eventually turn into moths or butterflies. In spite of their performance as small animated muffs; in spite of being the subject of numerous superstitions concerning winter weather; in spite of their unexpected appearance on the cold basement floor—in spite of all these anomalous attributes, woolly bears evolve into something rather dull. For the seventh time I look the answer up: into small-to-medium-sized undistinguished white-to-greyish moths called Arctiid moths. No wonder they are reluctant to make the trip.

## 🐛 4 🐛

DOWN IN THE HOLLOWS, in what we call the "coves" of the mountains, it is always spring. Water runs everywhere, even in the drought of August, even under the freezing moon of January, and there is a hopeful freshness and wetness to the air that speaks of spring. One day before Christmas I go down into one of these drains to get some hemlock cones for a wreath for my door. Almost everything in sight is evergreen—hemlock and pines and hollies, laurel and rhododendron, arbutus and wild ginger and partridge berry, Christmas fern and ground pine and wintergreen, mosses and lichens.

The witch hazel is bare, but it is blooming, covered with fringy yellow blossoms and surrounded by their strange non-scent, as though every smell but that of cleanliness had been washed away.

The big-leaved magnolia has dropped its foliage too, and the woods are strewn with two-foot-long leaves of a curious newspaper-grey. The upper side is a warm golden brown, but something in the leaf's boat shape causes it to land nine times out of ten with its underside uppermost. Until the leaves blend in with the rest of the compost, the woods have a littered and garbagy look.

Now on this chilly drizzling day I have come slipping and sliding down the steep rocky path, out of the winter woods, spare and bony and dry, into this semitropical garden along the creeks. It is the birds which most clearly indicate the season—kinglets and white-throated sparrows and purple finches. But even the birds sense that April promise, and suddenly the kinglets flash their ruby crowns; above the gurgle of water they burst suddenly into that astonishing song, too big by far to issue from this tiny creature and flowering sweetly on this springtime air.

## 5

IF A SPARROW COME before my window, I do not take part in its existence and pick about the gravel. I have no genius and no effort of will or discipline of mind can give me the slightest glimmering of what it is like to be a sparrow. I can only look and admire. Few other perching birds are so subtly and beautifully marked, the rich chestnuts and russets and creams softened with greys and tans and olives, all narrowly penciled with black. The backs of white-throated and chipping and song sparrows, even purple finches, are marvelously camouflaged as they feed on the ground under my window. It is astonishing how all the glory of those leaflike, almost paisley designs and patterns disappears and blends into the earth.

Among the birds that come to my feeder in the winter are some of the brightest and most exotically colored—cardinals and blue jays and evening grosbeaks and pine warblers, the greenest bird. In any weather they decorate the cedars and the laurel and in snow their glitter and dazzle are as gaudy as a Christmas card. A lovely sight, and yet in my heart I prefer the gentler colors—the patinaed bronze of winter goldfinches; the soft fawn of female cardinals with its underlying shadow of green and its overlying reflection of red; the slate of nuthatches.

And most of all it delights me to look down from my window to see a tracery of dead twigs and fallen oak leaves turn in a moment into a flock of sparrows in all their delicate and beautiful disguise.

# ⚔ 6 ⚔

WHEN MY CHILDREN were young we used to have for Christmas a cedar tree so big it was designated a "Sunday-school tree" and it generally managed to make a hole in the ceiling. Setting it up was always a miracle of engineering, involving clotheslines, a vast number of ropes and nails and heavy objects.

Now, we do not indulge in such nonsense. I am thinking of buying one of those trees made of some chemical, whose branches detach and can be folded away and saved from year to year. So much more sensible, so much easier an arrangement.

And yet I could never get over some awed atavistic pleasure in bringing a whole, great, still-living tree into the house, the marvel of it, the fragrance, the wonder of its seaweed foliage.

A good deal more than a tree came in: orange fungus and grey lichens, sometimes the pale fringed lichen called usnea moss, wasp galls, the shaggy cones of bagworms, and birds' nests. And once a white-footed mouse's nest filled with a hoard of withered dogwood berries and brier berries and one small acorn.

# *January*

## ⚡ 1 ⚡

WE WENT FIFTY MILES across the Cumberland Plateau to another wildlife refuge at Woods Reservoir. It is strangely different from and strangely the same as the one on our side of the mountain. Grebes there are more likely to be horned grebes than pied-billed, herons and geese are far less frequent and deer are more so. Yet the water and the hills and the homely voices of mallards are unchanged.

It was a bitter day. Ice held the edges of the lake in unnatural stillness. The coots walked disconsolately over the ice on their big green feet or shuffled uneasily along the hillsides. Pintails grazed in the fields.

I got out of the car near a graveled boat approach and across the way a boy wearing a sweatshirt lettered with the name of a local engineering college leaned against a jeep, dangling a plumb bob from his hand.

It takes a little while to get my telescope set up properly; the boy came over to see and we smiled and nodded, and at last he asked, "What you looking at?" And I answered, "The birds."

"Y'are?" he cried. "Looking at the *birds?* You're a *bird watcher!*"

There isn't much to say to this. A little group of hooded mergansers twinkled over and on a sand bar mallards slept; in the pale light their round breasts were like a clutter of rosy stones.

"Gee," said the boy, "I never saw anybody watch birds before!"

The dark cedars trickled down the tatty hills and against the white sky the mountains were colored the odd oblique colors of winter, crimson and blue and purple, colors that must be discerned, bright but not obvious. I offered the boy a look through the telescope. "Oh, yeah, the little dark things. There are a lot of 'em on the lake. All the time."

A red-tailed hawk soared slowly over the water and a harrier ran among the widgeon. A ruddy duck with its finned tail straight up behind it trudged from one sand bar toward another.

"I just didn't know there really was a bird watcher around here," the boy went on. "You're the first bird watcher I ever saw."

I could not think of anything to say. Gulls floated overhead and a flicker undulated his way underneath them. Something that might have been a gallinule rocked among the coots, a shoveler stood half-hidden by a stump on the far shore, the ruddy duck, having reached its sand bar, turned around to trudge back the way it had come. The boy observed me with some care.

Perhaps from another vantage point I could make sure about the gallinule, view the shoveler more distinctly, see what the widgeon were up to. I lifted the telescope, bunching its long legs together, and stowed it in the back seat of the car.

I said good-by uncomfortably. "Good-by," he answered, and then suddenly took a step closer. "Gee," he said and his voice was joyful, "I never saw a bird watcher before!"

We drove away. I felt fragile and depressed, a last surviving member of a species threatened with extinction.

## ⚹ 2 ⚹

WE MADE A ROUGH TRELLIS for the clematis to climb on—a pole with one crosspiece. The carpenter bee found it right away and used the crosspiece for a nest. All summer long when I worked in the yard I could hear those infinitesimal jaws gnawing away. As far away as twenty feet I could hear it.

The other day in a moment of whimsy I took down the crosspiece and sawed it open. I don't know what xpected to find in those silk-smooth chambers. Eggs? Larvae? Nothing at all? What I found were five fat queens, five gold-and-black sleeping beauties, waiting for he kiss of no particular prince, for they were already ertilized, waiting only for warm weather.

I was horrified and bound the whole business up with bicycle tape and left it on the window sill in the garage. n the spring four of them emerged. The fifth never woke, ut I don't believe I was the cause of her death.

The carpenter bees mumble around the house all ummer looking for nesting sites. I don't know what the equirements are or why the clematis trellis proved better han something else. They spent a long time inspecting he lintel and jambs of the back door but rejected that ocation. Anyway, the lintel was already occupied by arpenter ants, and has been as far back as we've lived ere. Sometimes they swarm, a flock of huge winged ants, nside and outside the house. Once I called the extermi- ators, but the sight of all that long dying repelled me, nd I have not done it since. After the exterminators had one their work, I thought the ants must all be gone, ut six months later there was a little pile of sawdust nder the lintel. I watched and by and by an ant came ut of a crack, walked to the edge of the lintel, leaned ver, and dropped a wood chip that antipodean distance the floor. They are still busy there, but we live in olerance. The swarms have never returned to anything ke their size before the exterminators; nowadays I prop he doors open and let them fly.

## ❧ 3 ❧

AFTER THE FIRST of the year the gulls, mostly herrin
gulls and ring-bills, gather in huge numbers alon
the river and the lakes, congregating along sand bars an
especially around the dams, around the spills where fi
come to eat the scraps of lunch thrown in by fisherme
and picnickers. The gulls eat anything, the fish, th
scraps, bait, paper, string—anything.

Sometimes I go to watch this scene, the huge whi
birds sailing and diving, the turbulent water, the sile
wall of the dam. Once standing there watching, I becar
aware of a crow sitting in a tree, also observing. After
few minutes he flew down low over the water's surfa
and when he came back to his perch he had in his b
a little flapping silver fish! Something he had learn
from the gulls? It must have been. He sat in his tr
grinning, obviously no end pleased with himself, and
thought he deserved to be.

## ❧ 4 ❧

PURPLE FINCHES come to my window feeder late in t
winter. They are greedy birds, consuming pounds a
pounds of sunflower seed, shoving other birds aside, a

quabbling briskly in small descending musical trills, like
unning your thumb along the teeth of a metallic comb.

Almost always the first to arrive are males. They are
ariously shaded, not purple, but rose-red. The rump
atch is the deepest and most intense color, a vivid cerise.
Contrastingly their heads are duller and drabber, the bill
eavy and the cheeks dark, giving their faces a sullen
ook. I am reminded of Marshal Foch's remark on being
aken to see the Folies-Bergère: "I never saw such sad
aces or such gay behinds. . . ."

## ₤ 5 ₤

WE LIVE "north of the river." The Tennessee River,
which takes a most tortuous course, runs north to
outh, so properly we are west of it. But here among the
nountains it is changing its route, bending in and out so
hat eventually it will run south to north. So perhaps we
ve east of the river. It is called "north of the river" by
ne and all. Whatever the location, however, it is on the
pposite bank from the part of the goose reserve where I
ke to go and watch.

When I come down off the mountain I can use one
f the bridges into the city and take the highway up the
south" side of the river. Or I can stay on my side and
ross to the reserve on a ferry. The ferry is unreliable
o in general I cross on the bridges. But I like ferries;
nce in a while I take a chance and cross on this one.

The passage lasts ten minutes or so. The man who fasten the chain across the ends of the barge, to keep us a from sliding in, remembers when it was otherwise. B fore the TVA built its dams and the water backing u in the reservoirs widened the river here to nearly twic its former extent. "Before the Goddamned TVA, didn take five minutes to cross here," he says in irritation. cannot fathom the reason for his acrimony, since th trip is only made twenty or so times a day and the re of the time he amuses himself with desultory fishing.

He is a toothless ancient, with incredibly dirty broke nails, a great liar. The trip is certainly not long enoug for him to finish regaling me with tales of enormous fis he has caught, of game he has shot when nobody els could find so much as a chipmunk to shoot, of his prowe with trotline and net and even his bare hands.

He is full of contempt for the warden in charge of th reserve. "Him!" he says derisively. "He don't know abou hunting, he just knows about corn." Something occurs him. "I'm a game warden. I'm a Fed. I'm over *him* Now he has a new tactic. He tells of the many times h has tricked hunters into illegal shooting . . . "and the I just th'owed back my jacket and showed my badge. . . He watches me slyly. I never know how much I a supposed to believe and how much I am supposed admire his powers of creation.

We are nearing the shore. Coots and black duck bounce in the water. Close to the end of the island a fe geese have gathered. " 'Em ole geese," he says, changin the subject. "They know when the season's over. Rig next day after, they come down here where anybody could shoot 'em. Don't see a single goose this close during the season. But right next day they come down. . . ."

He may be lying, but not altogether. The geese do seem to know almost at once that it is safe to come close to shore, to feed along the banks, to let humans approach nearer. And though I scarcely glimpse a deer during deer season, a week after the closing date they are grazing like cattle along the roadsides. And if the car stops to watch, they wait long enough to stare back before leaping away into the underbrush.

## ⚜ 6 ⚜

THE NUTHATCH CAME to the bird feeder and took away a sunflower seed and hung herself upside down on the trunk of an oak tree in order to wedge the seed into the bark and hatch it open. And suddenly her mate flew up and landed close to her, too close, so that she was startled and jostled and dropped the seed. They both ran up and down the oak tree as if looking for the lost treasure. And then he flew to the feeder and picked up another sunflower seed and flew back and handed it to her.

# *February*

---

## ❧ 1 ❧

IT IS A CURIOUS FACT that people think of ducks
clumsy and ridiculous, one of God's dimmer-witte
jokes. I suppose what they have in mind is domest
ducks, the barnyard Pekings.

For nothing could be more elegant than a pintail, the
a hooded merganser. A wood duck has the enamel
intricacy of a Fabergé jewel.

On the way back from the wildfowl refuge we pass
small lake, and so far we've never been disappointe
there's always at least one pair of buffleheads on it. T
lake is surrounded by pine trees. Their shadows dark
its surface, and on that black water the ducks flash bla

and white, black and white. In early spring the males rush at each other and crest their round white heads, twinkle in flight, fly and land, form patterns of two and three and four displaying males, almost as though it were deliberate, as if they knew how handsome they were.

Is this what artists are up to? I ask myself, not having been made privy to any such secrets. Is this what artists are trying to show me?

## ꙮ 2 ꙮ

SOMETIMES I SEE a bald eagle at the wildfowl reserve. Sometimes it is soaring over the pines, an imperial bird, crowned, lordly, stern ruler of some cloud-kingdom. And sometimes it is standing on a sand bar eating a dead fish, diminished to a rival carrion-eater by the crows who stand around it making raucous remarks. Nevertheless, they themselves are dwindled to grackle size by the eagle's hugeness, and they keep a respectful distance.

But once, and once only, I saw there a golden eagle, a vast dark bird shawled in brass. It too sat on a sand bar and ate dead fish, for it too scavenges. Yet it is also a fierce predator, can strike and carry away young and grown birds of every variety, even raccoons and foxes.

The whole place knew it. When the eagle rose and flew over a grove of cedars, suddenly the world erupted with crows, herons, jays—screaming, wheeling, circling, crying with fear. I have never, before or since, seen such a terrible sky, so filled with anger and dread.

# ⚔ 3 ⚔

WHEN IT SNOWS, in the thin layer under the eaves th
birds leave tracks, and if it is so cold that ice crust
the snow, there will be blood stains in those small starr
marks, rose-colored tracks in the white snow. I am fasci
nated by this bleak sight, the stuff of legend. And it i
in this region a rare sight fortunately, not only for th
feet of sparrows but also for me, who might grow inure
to its poignant magic. Tracks of any kind are rare, as
matter of fact. In the woods, wet or dry, only a heav
animal leaves prints. A deer, for instance, and it is dee
tracks I see most often, or those of a big dog. In cleare
places along the edges of streams or lakes, in mud o
sand, in places where a June bug can and sometime
does leave a trail, I long to be an expert, one of thos
loreful people who can tell a deer mouse's trace from
shrew's. Whose claws dipped here? Who padded awa
there? Deer are easy, like nothing else except perhap
pigs, which generally don't run loose here. Dogs are eas
if they are big; we have no wolves. But a smaller dog-
could it be a fox? Couldn't it?

Raccoons have such childish small hands and fee
sturdy and appealing. A mussel leaves a long narrow tra
at the water's edge. Herons' big stalking prints dwarf th
crows' tracks, which in turn make miniatures of perch

ng birds'. There is something eerie about the delicate
nobby-fingered marks of possums, with those curious
wide palms and back-sloping thumbs.

Here is something I am almost certain is a squirrel,
and that might be a land tortoise. I have to go far afield
to see these things, and hardly ever see more than two
kinds at the edge of the same pool. Here there is enough
water so that we can, for the most part, demand privacy
from each other when we hunt and drink. Besides, there
are likely a good many signs that I don't recognize.

One thing I do always recognize and by which I never
fail to be astonished: my own tracks, my own shod feet,
headed the way I am now an hour later coming back,
yet each one in a different river.

## ⚑ 4 ⚑

RIDING ALONG the river road with my husband, I
looked up the mountainside and there they were—
five young bucks posed and poised on the rocks. We
stopped to watch, and the deer stared back with that
curious combination of insolence and timidity that is their
hallmark. They twitched their ears nervously, looking at
one another for suggestions or reassurance, and then at
last scrambled farther up the hill.

Change is the necessary and vital element in any landscape, the slow change of growth and decay, of erosion
and deposit. Sometimes the change is quick and violent,

wind or lightning, flood or fire, or the hard-clankir
machines of men.

And yet the sun rises every morning at its appointe
hour, the seasons follow inexorably one upon the othe
and the water thrush returns each March, punctual a
most to the day.

The next year, riding along the river with my husban
I said, "It was just there we saw them . . ." And the
they were, five young bucks poised and posed among t
rocks.

## 5

THE TVA DROPS the water in its dams during t
winter, waiting for the rains of late February a
March. The river dwindles and its bare bones stick o
Along the banks, fish and other aquatic creatures fa
occasional victim to this precaution, trapped in poo
Over the desert of exposed river bottom, crows, starlin,
gulls, and other creatures scavenge.

And once I came on half a hundred black vultu
feasting on this bounty. As they ate they talked, a stran
conversation of hisses and whispery growls and sepulch
croaks. It was the only time I had ever heard th
creatures make a sound.

A vulture in the air is beautiful, but on the grou
it becomes a wonderfully ugly beast—hunched, ba

rtive, graceless. I was pleased to find that their voices
lso had two aspects—the harshness and hoarseness over-
id with a gentle susurration, a soothing, almost grateful
uality—the voices of gravediggers.

# *March* 11

## ☙ 3 ☙

Any warmish day in December or January the cho
frogs may call. Birds sing for a number of reaso
to attract a mate; to establish a territory, and warn aw
other birds; to communicate; or simply for singing's sa
But frogs sing for one reason only, and what they are s
ing over and over is "Sex! Sex! Sex!" At least accordi
to Archie Carr, a writer who should know.

It makes a lovely song, a sweet, slow-rising trill.
charming small hymn to procreation. On one of th
days I can stand on the edge of the mountain and h
it floating up from every pond and puddle. By the e
of March the ponds and puddles are full of eggs, teemi

with tadpoles, who have a good chance of avoiding death by freezing, if not by any other means available.

I can waste a good deal of time poking about in the edges of shallow ponds, catching cold and water beetles, hoping to stir up a salamander or a small Loch Ness monster, falling in, creating havoc in the mud. I can never resist; something mysterious is hidden under the layers of dead leaves and silt. When the eggs are laid and the tadpoles begin to grow, I am more drawn than ever and hunker down to watch it happen. And one morning in the middle of March there are the leopard frogs fringing the edge of the water, slender males each clutching his fat female in pop-eyed single-mindedness. Sometimes his embrace is so passionate and long that the lady drowns; he has even been known to drown himself. There is a moral lesson to be learned here, but whether about sex or single-mindedness I have not yet determined.

## ⚔ 4 ⚔

THE CAT CAUGHT a cotton rat and brought it home to her kittens, forgetting in her moment of excitement that kittens, like the Duchess's smiles, all stopped together.

The cotton rat was just the size and shape and heft of a good comfortable kitten; and the cat, perhaps in confusion, carried it about and licked it and loved it till I grew sick of the spectacle and took it away from her. In the palm of my hand it lies limp and damp, its eyes

open, its neck broken, the marks of claws in its skull
In death, like all rodents, it is a particularly forlorn
sight; there is something infinitely pathetic about thos
two projecting teeth. In life, in spite of the grizzled
rather harsh fur, it is an endearing creature, not so engag
ing as a vole perhaps, but more so than hamsters and
gerbils. I wonder if cotton rats would adapt to caging
and domestication. The thought is a little intimidating
for they are among the world's most prolific beasts, often
breeding right through the year and producing vast litter
at frequent intervals; "their numbers," to quote an au
thority, ". . . surpassing that of all other mammals pu
together in the areas where the environment suits their
tastes."

In the secret world of grass stems then, in the runnel
and tunnels of earth and among the fallen branches an
the stones and bones and rubble of the gulleys, they mu
live by the million. Just outside my door there must b
thousands: cotton rats as big as my fist, voles and shrew
hardly bigger than my little finger—a teeming populac
constantly in search of food, going, coming, quarrelin
mating, borning, dying.

Yet if the cat does not catch one and bring it home
I can go months, even years, without laying eyes on on
of them. Animals who exist almost solely to feed othe
animals must of necessity lead so arcane an existenc
swift and silent and dim, in the shadows even at noo

I see them most often in the fall, somehow, when th
vegetation is gone and still the weather tempts them
activity. In the November twilight a cotton rat go

barreling down the slopes. Sitting at my typewriter, I can see a small scuttling shape, a shrew, cross the driveway and disappear between the roots of a pine. Among the twigs and flakes of bark and moss, the entrance to its hole is so beautifully disguised I cannot see it at all, though I know it is there, and must put my hand on the ground and discover the little portal with my fingers.

## 5

THE DOG HAS HAD spring fever and for two days would not eat his dinner. I dumped it out on the grass, a stale mixture of Friskies and table scraps, milk and dog biscuit. In ten minutes the starlings found it and waded in. Oh, the chuckling delight of it, to be belly-deep in food. It is one of their few charms, this forthright and exuberant pleasure in whatever the moment offers. The jay will come slyly and snatch a furtive bite and go off shrieking his thievery. The mockingbird is somehow resentful—where was this bounty in the starving days of January?

But the starling merely rejoices. Enjoy! Enjoy!

I am fond of starlings, those Philistines among birds. For the name if nothing else—Easterling, the traveler from the East. For their plumage—bespangled and tinseled as a trapeze artist's costume. For their cheerfully strident whistles and strange mocking calls, for one that is the far-off, nostalgia-drenched, early-morning cry of a

rooster, and no well-bred rooster at that, but a rusty
voiced, droop-tailed mongrel scratching the dusty edge
of a country road.

Everything about them is graceless and vulgar, the
stumpy, almost tailless, awkward bodies, the wide wings
the great, ugly yellow bill. They walk as though they
had on bedroom slippers several sizes too big, lifting
their feet high and spreading their toes to keep the slippers from falling off. They are clumsy fliers, whirring
those stubby wings desperately, looking always as though
they were going to fall short of their goal.

But they are champion gliders, spreading their kite
shaped bodies on the air, and sailing sailing sailing
surely and beautifully, up down up down down down
a wonderful thing to watch.

## ⚝ 6 ⚝

I WENT UP to the wildfowl reserve, to say good-by to
the geese. We chose the right day, blue and bright
and the geese were there by the hundred. They were
restless and active, flying up and landing, walking about
with that proud long-legged walk, calling and calling
The geese make three sounds, their beautiful wild voice
the booming roar of their wings in flight, and the silken
hiss when their bodies slide into the water. And on the
day of farewell, I heard all three.

There is a field where the marsh hawks quarter and

oday the geese are feeding there, with the sun on their bronze backs, and one pintail in the midst of them. Among the birds on the water there were three blue geese and one snow, as there often are. Their white heads and necks make a startling contrast with the black ones of the Canadas. They are handsome creatures but they do not have the appeal for me that the Canadas have; there is something placid and domestic about them, those pink bills and feet; their voices are not so deeply fierce and beautiful.

Killdees and one snipe pattered around on the sand bars, the trees crackled and sparkled with redwings, frogs called from the hollows, and the plowed fields were starred and spangled with chickweed and dandelions and ranunculus. We ate our lunch away from the water, out of the cold wind, and a woodchuck watched us from behind a kind of rampart it had erected in front of the entrance of its burrow. A number of young bulls grazing in the field next to us, rushed down to the fence with brave looks and lowered heads, but when I went up to them and offered the core of my apple and the crust of a sandwich, they retreated in disorder. At the far end of their pasture a deer leaped over the fence, scampered across the corner of the meadow, leaped out again, and disappeared into the pines. If they envied him they did not show it, following his progress with the same earnest thoughtfulness which they had devoted to my consumption of a hard-boiled egg.

There was no sound but the wind and the geese and a far-away barking dog.

It has been a good day. Time and chance happeneth to us all. All sorts of imponderables lie between here and October, between here and Canada. But whatever happens, I have had this good day in which to say good-by to the geese.

# *Afterword*

AMONG MY EARLIEST recollections is of myself standing transfixed by the song of a Bewick's wren. What it was, I did not at age four know or care. I recognized it simply as the essence of an April morning.

From the wren I went on to more momentous occasions. I marked my days by Events, by the sight of wild turkeys rising above a little dark copse of pines; by the seldom-heard calls of chuck-will's-widows; by my first clear close look at ibises; by the spine-chilling sensation of a snake moving unexpectedly under my unwary hand.

As I grow older I find myself returning to the less sophisticated attitudes of four years old. More and homelier things, the stems of grasses and the songs of crickets, seem to me miraculous.

Life, in order to continue, must be at least endurable to its participants. But that it is possible, in spite of implicit horrors, to find it beautiful fills me with astonishment, with gratitude. What I have hoped to convey in these pages is my own sense of how valuable and how fragile it is, this tiny spark in an eternity of darkness, and how greatly to be treasured in whatever manifestation.

FPT  ISBN 0-688-00992-1          >>$6.50

"This quiet and gentle book is a nature lover's delight . . . and joins the ranks of the classics of this field."

—*Library Journal*

# The Living Year

### An
## Almanac for My Survivors
# Mary Q. Steele

*The Living Year* is for all those who celebrate nature's miracles in their own backyards, gardens, local fields and forests, even basements.

A housewife and well-known children's author, who is a gifted naturalist and bird watcher, has turned her incredibly discerning eye to the life around her home in Signal Mountain, Tennessee. Mary Q. Steele's flora range from humble weeds to a captive ailanthus tree; her fauna from a voracious Chinese mantis to a golden eagle. Sensitive but never sentimental, her chronicle delights in nature's beauty without neglecting the cruelty of nature and the callousness of humans. It has been selected by the Natural History Book Club.

Mary Q. Steele's fellow homespun naturalists will love *The Living Year* and will welcome it as a gift.

*Cover design by Barbara Singer*

QUILL/105 Madison Avenue/New York, N.Y. 10016

5F7